Ramen Cookbook

Quick and Easy Japanese Noodle Recipes for Everyday to Make with Local Ingredients

MAGGIE BARTON

CONTENTS

MEDIUM – 30/90 MINUTES

HARD – 90+ MINUTES 151

EASY – 15/30 MINUTES

MISO RAMEN SOUP

INGREDIENTS FOR 2 PORTIONS

- 4 mushrooms (fresh or dried shiitake mushrooms)
- 2 spring onions
- ¼ sheet of nori sheets
- 100g of tofu for soups
- 50g of bean sprouts
- 100g of noodles (ramen or other egg-free asian noodles for noodle soup)
- 2 cloves of garlic
- 1 tbsp. Of oil (neutral)
- ¼ tbsp. Of chili flakes
- 600ml of vegetable stock
- 2 tbsp. Of miso

PREPARATION

Total time: approx. 15 minutes

1. Soak the dried shiitake mushrooms in a little water for approx. 1/2 hour, and then bring to a boil briefly, let cool and cut into strips. Only cut fresh shiitake into strips. Cut the spring onions into fine rings, the nori into strips, and the tofu into cubes.

2. Chop the garlic and fry in the vegetable oil. Before it turns brown, add miso and chili flakes and pour in the vegetable stock.

3. Cook the ramen or other pasta al dente in boiling water according to the package. Then drain well and spread it over two large soup bowls. Fill up with the miso broth and garnish with shiitake mushrooms, spring onions, bean sprouts, tofu and nori strips.

MISO SOUP

INGREDIENTS FOR 2 PORTIONS

- 600ml of water
- Dashi (instant, amount according to the package for 2 servings)
- 2 tbsp of spice paste (miso, light)
- 100g of tofu (in small cubes)
- 2 spring onions (cut into rings)
- 10 sheets of wakame (dried)
- 6 mushrooms (shiitake, dried, cut into fine strips)
- 100g of salmon fillet (alternatively beef fillet, in fine strips)
- 100g of noodles [japanese (udon, soba, etc.) Cooked, possibly shredded]
- 1 tbsp of chives
- Fish sauce or soy sauce
- 1 egg (whisked, at will)

PREPARATION

Total time: approx. 20 minutes

1. Heat the water with dashi in a larger saucepan; add the tofu cubes and shiitake strips (it is best to cut them with scissors). And let them cook for about 10 minutes. Add onion rings and simmer for another 5 minutes. Add salmon fillet or beef fillet strips and the whisked eggs as desired, cook for 2-3 minutes.

2. Stir in miso paste with a little soup and add cooked noodles and Wakame leaves to the soup, then boil it again. Season to taste and serve sprinkled with chives.

3. Fish stock can also be used instead of water and dashi. For taste reasons, I would only use vegetable or meat broth in an emergency - it is a fish-soy-based soup.

4. The individual insoles can be varied or left out. With all the trimmings, you get a stew that goes as the main course; only with tofu, shiitake, spring onions, egg and/or Wakame can the soup be served very well as part of a Japanese meal. As a warm addition to sushi, the 'stripped down' soup also tastes very good.

TRADITIONAL MISO RAMEN

INGREDIENTS FOR 1 PORTION

- 100g of ramen noodles or chinese noodles without eggs
- Oil
- 1 glove of garlic
- Sambal oelek or chili
- 200ml of broth
- 2 tbsp. Of miso paste
- ½ glass of mung bean sprouts
- 2 small disc of roast pork (cooked)
- 3 surimi-stäbchen
- ½ small dose of corn
- Spinach leaves, thawed (portioned) or 2 seaweed leaves
- 1 spring onion

PREPARATION

Total time: approx. 15 minutes

1. Cook ramen noodles according to the package instructions.

2. Heat the oil in the saucepan. Add garlic and sambal oelek. Before it turns brown, add the broth and stir in the miso paste.

3. Rinse the mung bean seedlings with water and put them briefly in the broth, as well as the roast pork and the Surimi sticks, so that they become warm.

4. Cut the spring onions into small pieces.

5. Place the noodles in a large bowl; arrange everything in a circle except the spring onions. Pour in the broth from the center (let it get really hot again beforehand). Finally, put the spring onions in the middle.

Note:

- This soup can also be modified and, for example, topped with half an egg, broccoli, mushrooms or the likes can be used.

FAST MISO RAMEN

INGREDIENTS FOR 4 PORTIONS

- 1 onion
- 2 cloves of garlic
- 1 piece of ginger
- Soy sauce
- Rice wine (optional)
- 2 liters of vegetable broth or chicken broth
- Miso paste (approx. 1 - 2 tbsp.)
- 300g of ramen noodles without egg
- Oil for frying
- For the topping:
- 1 spring onions
- Some mushrooms
- 250g of chicken breast
- Sesame oil
- Chili flakes
- 4 eggs

PREPARATION

Total time: approx. 30 minutes

1. Cut the onion, ginger, and garlic very finely and fry in a saucepan with a little oil. Deglaze with soy sauce and broth and bring to a simmer. Add the miso paste - preferably through a small sieve, as it will not dissolve easily. Season with a little rice wine and soy sauce. The broth can be used directly or continue to simmer for 10 to 20 minutes.

2. Cook the pasta separately according to the package instructions. Do not add to the broth.

3. Now prepare the toppings. Cut the spring onion. Clean and fry the mushrooms. Marinate the chicken breast with soy sauce and oil, then fry. Boil the eggs for 7 minutes and then put them in ice water so that they are still soft when served.

4. Place the pasta in the serving bowls. Then pour in the broth and spread the toppings on it. The toppings can be varied at will, depending on what you have at home.

MISO UDON SOUP WITH SILK TOFU

INGREDIENTS FOR 4 PORTIONS

For the soup:

- 1½ liters of vegetable stock
- 6 tbsp of miso paste
- 3 tbsp of soy sauce
- 3 tbsp of agave nectar
- 2 tbsp of ginger
- 1 tbsp of algae (dried)
- 1 tbsp of garlic powder

Also: (for the insert)

- 400g udon noodles (thick)
- 300g of silken tofu
- 200g of broccoli florets
- 200g of spinach
- 2 spring onions
- 2 carrots

PREPARATION

Total time: approx. 20 minutes

1. Bring the soup ingredients to a boil in a saucepan except for the miso paste. Turn the stove down to medium temperature and stir in the miso paste.

2. Slice the carrots and add to the soup with the broccoli florets and cook for 5 minutes. Cut the silk tofu into pieces, add to the soup, and cook everything together for another 5 minutes.

3. In the last minute, stir in the spinach and spring onions, and spread everything on bowls.

FAST RAMEN NOODLES

INGREDIENTS FOR 2 PORTIONS

- 2 packs of ramen noodles, instant
- 2 spring onions

For the dressing:

- 2 tbsp of soy sauce
- 2 tbsp of chili flakes
- 1 tbsp of rice wine vinegar
- 1 tbsp of agave nectar

PREPARATION

Total time approx. 15 minutes

1. Cut the spring onions into slices and set the green part aside. Pour boiling water over the white portion and pasta and let it steep for 5 minutes. Then pour off.
2. Mix the ingredients for the dressing and stir it into the pasta. Divide it into 2 bowls and mix with the green part of the spring onions.

RAMEN NOODLES SOUP

INGREDIENTS FOR 4 PORTIONS

- 1 tbsp of sesame oil
- 1 shallot (in fine rings)
- 1 clove of garlic, finely chopped
- 100g of shiitake mushroom (in strips)
- 1 chili pepper (green, seeded, finely chopped)
- 1 stem of lemongrass (the inside, finely chopped)
- 1 liter of vegetable stock
- 3 tbsp of soy sauce (light)
- 150g of pasta (ramen)
- 100g of chinese cabbage (in fine strips)
- Coriander

PREPARATION

Total time: approx. 30 minutes

1. Let the oil warm up in a pan. Add the shallot and all ingredients up, including lemongrass and steam for about 3 minutes. Pour in the broth and soy sauce and bring to a boil. Add the Chinese cabbage and the noodles, cook for about 3 minutes until they are al dente.
2. Spread in soup bowls, garnish with a little coriander.

RAMEN NOODLES WITH CHICKEN

INGREDIENTS FOR 1 PORTION

- 1 handful of noodles (ramen noodles) or glass noodles
- 2 spring onions
- Chili powder
- Chicken breast fillet, or beef, cut into small pieces
- Beef broth, or chicken broth
- Sesame oil
- Soy sauce
- Rice vinegar

PREPARATION

Total time: approx. 20 minutes

1. Cook the pasta in salted water and drain.

2. Cut the spring onion into small rings and fry until translucent, then add the meat and cook.

3. Heat the broth, season with chili, soy sauce, and rice vinegar. Place the broth in a high bowl and put the noodles in so that they protrude above the broth. Carefully place the mixture from the pan over it and cut another spring onion into rings, put them on top. Pour sesame oil over it and serve.

FAST WANNABE RAMEN

INGREDIENTS FOR 1 PORTION

- 1 pack of noodles
- 1½ kg cop of plum wine, peach wine, or mirin (shot glass or egg cup full)
- 1 tbsp of miso paste, light
- 1½ tbsp of cane sugar
- 1 egg (cooked)
- 2 small sliced cucumber (snack cucumbers)
- 1 pinch of parsley (frozen, or fresh. If available, you can use chives or spring onions)
- Soy sauce
- Pepper
- Oil

PREPARATION

Total time: approx. 17 minutes

1. Put some amount of water in a saucepan according to the package, together with the miso paste, cane sugar (or normal sugar), plum wine, seasoning mix of the pasta (if included) and the cucumber. When the water starts to a boil, add the pasta and cook according to the length of the pack.

2. Prepare an appropriate bowl by adding a few dashes of soy sauce, a little pepper, and oil to the bottom of the bowl. Peel, halve and set the egg aside.

3. Put the finished pasta with the broth in the bowl, drape the egg on it and mix with a little parsley, chives or similar. Decorate (spring onions).

Note:

- The ingredients such as egg and the vegetables can be varied with z. B. strips of chicken, carrots, peas, scrambled eggs, or other.

SIMPLE RAMEN WITH PAK CHOI

INGREDIENTS FOR 1 PORTION

- 2 tbsp of chicken broth (instant)
- ½ liter of water (hot)
- Ginger
- 1 cloves of garlic
- 1½ tbsp of soy sauce
- 2 tbsp of mirin
- 100g mie noodles (instant)
- 1 pak of choi
- 5 mushrooms or other mushrooms
- 1 chicken breast fillet
- 1 egg

PREPARATION

Total time: approx. 30 minutes

1. Mix the chicken broth with the hot water. Cut the ginger and clove of garlic into small pieces and heat them in soy sauce and mirin. Boil the egg and cook the noodles in the chicken broth according to the package instructions.

2. Then pour the chicken broth with noodles through a sieve over soy sauce, mirin, ginger, and add a clove of garlic so that the two mixes together.

3. Cut the chicken breast fillet into approx. 1cm thick slices and fry in a little fat, soy sauce, and mirin. Chop the pak choi and mushrooms, and sweat them.

4. Place the noodles in a bowl, arrange the pak choi, mushrooms, the boiled halved egg, and chicken breast fillet on top, and pour the broth over it.

SPICY TANTANMEN RAMEN

INGREDIENTS FOR 2 PORTIONS

- 1 tbsp of olive oil or other oil
- 1 onion
- 1 carrot
- 2 cloves of garlic
- 4 shiitake mushrooms, dried
- 1 liter of water
- 1 tbsp of vegetable broth (instant)
- 1 tbsp of miso paste
- 1 pack of dashi powder
- 1 shot of almond milk (almond drink)
- 2 tbsp of tahini
- 2 tbsp of sambal oelek
- 2 tbsp of sesame oil
- 2 tbsp of soy sauce
- 2 pack of ramen noodles
- Sesame for sprinkling

PREPARATION

Total time: approx. 30 minutes

1. Soak the shiitake mushrooms in hot water for 5 minutes. In the meantime, cut the onion roughly so that you can still grasp it well with chopsticks (e.g. B. eighth).

2. Cut the carrots diagonally into long, 2mm thick slices. Peel the garlic and press on with the knife side.

3. Fry the shiitake mushrooms, onions, garlic, and carrots in a saucepan with oil on medium heat until they are light brown. A light brown layer should form on the bottom of the pot. Warning, don't let it go black!

4. Add the water and season with instant vegetable broth, miso paste, and dashi powder. If available, and season to taste. Let the soup simmer gently until the carrots are done.

5. In the meantime, cook and drain the pasta according to the package instructions.

6. Prepare 2 soup bowls until the noodles are ready. Whisk 1 teaspoon of sesame paste, 1 teaspoon of Sambal Oelek, 1 teaspoon of sesame oil, and 1 teaspoon of soy sauce with a whisk - by the way, this smells incredibly good.

7. Fish out the carrot slices and mushrooms out of the soup for decoration. Cut the mushrooms into strips.

8. Stir the dash of milk into the soup. Spread the soup on the 2 bowls and whisk well with the whisk. Add the pasta to the soup, decorate with carrots, mushrooms. and sesame seeds.

RAMEN NOODLES WITH PORK

INGREDIENTS FOR 4 PORTIONS

- 200g of pork
- 1 bar of leek
- 100g of mushrooms (shitake mushrooms)
- 50g of bean sprouts
- 1 piece of ginger (walnut-sized)
- 800ml of broth (miso broth, alternatively chicken broth)
- 250g of noodles (udon noodles)
- 1 chili
- Soy sauce
- ½ bundle of coriander

PREPARATION

Total time: approx. 20 minutes

1. Cut the pork and sear for approx. 5 minutes on both.

2. Cut the leek into rings, quarter the mushrooms, and shower off the sprouts. Finely chop the ginger and chili pepper, and bring to a boil in the broth with about 3 tablespoons of soy sauce. Then add the leek and cook over medium heat for about 10 minutes. Reduce the heat further and let the mushrooms and sprouts steep for another 5 minutes. Season again with soy sauce.

3. Boil the pasta than arrange the pasta and meat on plates or in bowls. Pour the soup over it and decorate with finely chopped coriander.

SPICY RAMEN SOUP WITH MUSHROOMS

INGREDIENTS FOR 3 PORTIONS

- 200g of tofu (japanese, fried)
- 2 liters of vegetable stock
- 2 tbsp of soy sauce
- 3 tbsp of sesame oil
- 1 onion
- 1 carrot
- ½ small cabbage
- 50g of peas, frozen
- 50g of shiitake mushroom
- 100g of bean sprouts
- 1 chili pepper (red)
- 4 tbsp of miso paste
- ½ tbsp of kampot pepper (red, freshly ground)
- ½ tbsp of pepper (black, freshly ground)
- 240g of ramen noodles

PREPARATION

Total time: approx. 35 minutes

1. Bring the vegetable broth to a boil with soy sauce and sesame oil, and cook the ramen noodles in the broth in 4 minutes. Take out and keep warm.

2. Peel the carrot, use a spiral cutter to make strips and shorten to 1cm. Cut pointed cabbage into narrow strips and shorten to 2cm. Peel the onion and cut it into cubes. Dice the shiitake mushrooms.

3. Cut the tofu into strips and fry in a pan without oil, remove and keep warm with the ramen noodles.

4. Cook the carrots, onions and pointed cabbage in the broth for 15 minutes. Now add the bean sprouts, shiitake mushrooms, and peas, then cook for another 5 minutes. Chop the chili finely and add to the broth with the pepper and bring to a boil.

5. Take the pot off the stove and stir the miso paste into the soup.

6. Spread the noodles on bowls, pour the soup over them and garnish with the tofu.

SPICY RAMEN NOODLES SOUP

INGREDIENTS FOR 2 PORTIONS

- 1 liter of chicken broth
- 1 stem of lemongrass
- 1 piece of ginger root
- 4 tbsp of soy sauce (approx. Plus something to taste)
- 80g of ramen noodles
- 300g of chinese cabbage
- 75g of sugar snap
- 1 spring onion
- Lemon juice

For the topping:

- Salt
- 1 of chili pepper (fresh, cut into thin rings)
- Some spring onion (cut into thin rings)
- Sesame

PREPARATION

Total time: approx. 30 minutes

1. Peel the ginger and chop very finely (it should be about 1 heaping tablespoon).

2. Cut the Chinese cabbage into fine strips, cut the pods in half, and cut the spring onions into rings. Halve the lower light part of the lemongrass lengthways.

3. Simmer broth, lemongrass, ginger and soy sauce in a saucepan for about 8-10 minutes. Add the ramen noodles and cook for 2 minutes. Add Chinese cabbage, sugar snap peas and spring onions, mix everything and cook for about 5 minutes.

4. Season with soy sauce, a little lemon juice, and a little salt if necessary and serve hot.

5. If you want, you can spread the soup on plates and sprinkle with fresh spring onion rings, chili rings and sesame seeds roasted dry in the pan.

JAPANESE RAMEN NOODLES SOUP

INGREDIENTS FOR 1 PORTION

- 500ml of water
- 2 tbsp of chicken broth powder (to taste)
- Soup noodles
- 2 eggs
- 1 handful of cherry tomatoes
- 1 shot of mirin (alternatively a little pinch of sugar)
- Soy sauce
- Butter or similar for roasting
- 1 nori sheet (crushed)

PREPARATION

Total time: approx. 15 minutes

1. Bring the water to a boil; add broth, vermicelli, mirin and soy sauce. Cut the nori sheet into small pieces, you can hold it a little over the warm stovetop, then it becomes brittle and you can easily crumble it. Put in the soup.

2. While the pasta is cooking (stir occasionally so that nothing sticks to the bottom of the pot), fry the eggs with a little butter in the pan over low heat as fried eggs. The eggs should be thorough, but ideally, the egg yolk should still be liquid. If you don't like it that way, you can, of course, fry the fried eggs even longer. Halve the tomatoes and briefly fry them in the pan.

3. When the noodles are soft enough, season the soup, and if necessary, season with soy sauce. Then put the soup in a bowl. As soon as the eggs are ready, carefully slide them into the soup with the tomatoes, if possible without damaging the egg yolk.

4. Depending on the dosage, the soy sauce and nori leaves can be quite flavor-intensive, so it is advisable to first take a little less of both and then season them if necessary.

SOBA NOODLES WITH TOFU

INGREDIENTS FOR 2 PORTIONS

- 250g of japanese noodles (soba noodles)
- 300g of tofu (sliced)
- 1 lemon, grated zest and 1 tablespoon of juice
- 3cm of ginger root (grated)
- 1 tbsp of syrup (agave syrup)
- 1 tbsp of cayenne pepper
- 1 tbsp of salt
- 1 shot of rice vinegar
- 1 shot of soy sauce
- 2 tbsp of sesame oil
- Coriander green, chopped
- 5 spring onions (cut into thin rings)
- ½ cucumber (seeded and cut into thin slices)
- ½ bell pepper (red, cut into thin slices)
- Sesame seeds, toasted

PREPARATION

Total time: approx. 20 minutes

1. Mix the lemon zest with the ginger, agave syrup, cayenne pepper and salt for the dressing. Add lemon juice, rice vinegar, and soy sauce and stir well. Add sesame oil and whip up the dressing with a mixing stick.

2. Cook the soba noodles until bite-proof and quench under cold water. Fry the tofu brown on both sides in a cast iron grill pan, and briefly fry the peppers.

3. Mix the soba noodles with coriander, spring onions, bell pepper, cucumber and 2/3 of the dressing. Spread on two plates, place tofu on each, drizzle with the remaining dressing and sprinkle with sesame.

4. All kinds of salad go well with this.

SOBA WITH VEGETABLES

INGREDIENTS FOR 2 PORTIONS

- 250g of noodles, soba noodles (japanese buckwheat noodles)
- 500g of mixed vegetables, frozen (e.g. Peas and carrots)
- 200ml of water
- 1 tbsp of ginger powder
- 5 tbsp of soy sauce
- Lemongrass, to taste
- 1 tbsp of cumin
- 2 tbsp of spice mix (chinese 5-spice powder)
- Salt and pepper (to taste)
- 1 tbsp of berries (red pepper berries)

PREPARATION

Total time: approx. 15 minutes

1. Place the frozen vegetables with the spices and water on the stove and cook.

2. At the same time, cook the pasta in plenty of salted water according to the package instructions.

3. Drain the pasta in a sieve and add to the vegetables. Mix well and serve.

SOBA NOODLES WITH PAK CHOI AND MUSHROOMS

INGREDIENTS FOR 3 PORTIONS

- 150g of Soba Noodles (Japanese Buckwheat Noodles)
- 3 cups of water
- 300g of Pak choi
- 5 large Mushrooms (brown)
- 1 large Onion
- 3 tbsp of hoisin sauce
- 1 tbsp of teriyaki sauce
- 1 tbsp of fish sauce
- ½ tbsp of Paprika powder (noble sweet)
- ½ tbsp of Pepper (ground)
- Salt
- Chili powder
- 100ml of water
- 1 tbsp of Sesame oil or other oil

PREPARATION

Total time: approx. 30 minutes

1. First, bring the 3 cups of water to a boil in a saucepan, reduce the heat and simmer the soba noodles in them according to the package. Pour into a colander and spray cold. Put aside.

2. Peel the onion and cut it into medium-sized cubes. Wash the pak choi and cut it into strips about 1.5cm wide. Set the leaves aside separately from the stems. Clean the mushrooms and cut them into strips about 0.5cm wide.

3. Heat the sesame oil in a wok. Add onions and stir-fry for about 2 minutes. Add the teriyaki and fish sauce and stir well. Then add the cut stalks from the Pak Choi and let it cook for 2 minutes. Then add the mushrooms and stew for another 3 minutes.

4. Then add approx. 100ml of water and stir well with the hoisin sauce. With the paprika powder, pepper and salt, who like to taste hearty chili powder. Add the drained soba noodles and mix everything well. Let it warm up.

5. The dish can be prepared for vegetarian if the fish sauce is omitted.

SOBA NOODLES WITH LIME AND PEANUT DRESSING

INGREDIENTS FOR 2 PORTIONS

- 225g of pasta (soba), optionally another type of pasta
- 2 pak choi (or savoy cabbage or swiss chard)
- 1 small cucumber
- 1 lime
- 2 spring onions
- 1 clove of garlic
- 1 bunch mint
- 50g of peanuts
- 6 tbsp of soy sauce
- 30g of peanut butter
- 20g of honey
- 1 chili pepper (dried)
- 1 tbsp of vegetable oil

PREPARATION

Total time: approx. 20 minutes

1. Rub the peel of the lime, squeeze out the lime. Finely chop the peanuts. Finely dice the garlic.

2. Place the soy sauce with peanut butter, add half of the peanuts, the grated lime peel, and the juice of the squeezed lime, honey, garlic, chili and oil in a tall vessel and mash them finely with a mixing stick. Season with salt and pepper to taste.

3. Wash the pak choi, remove the stalk and cut into bite-size pieces. Cut the spring onions into fine rings. Finely chop the mint leaves. Quarter the cucumber lengthways and cut into 5mm pieces.

4. Cook the pasta according to the package instructions. Then put the Pak Choi in the pot and let everything soak in the water for a minute. Drain the soba noodles with pak choi and mix with the peanut dressing in the pot used previously. Add the spring onions, cucumber, remaining peanuts, and mint to the saucepan and stir.

YAKISOBA WITH VEGETABLES

INGREDIENTS FOR 2 PORTIONS

- 1 pack of noodles, wide (japanese wheat noodles)
- 1 pack of butter vegetables (frozen)
- Soy sauce or mushroom or teriyaki sauce (asia shop)

PREPARATION

Total time: approx. 15 minutes

1. Cook the pasta according to the package instructions.

2. Put the buttered vegetables in a saucepan and cook.

3. Arrange the pasta on a deep plate, spread the buttered vegetables on top and drizzle with the sauces to taste.

YAKISOBA WITH SHRIMPS

INGREDIENTS FOR 4 PORTIONS

- 500g of japanese noodle, yakisoba noodle (wheat noodle, not buckwheat noodle)
- 200g of cut pork or chicken (into 4 cm pieces)
- 150g of shrimp (washed, deveined, peeled)
- 250g of white cabbage (cut in julienne)
- 1 carrot (cut into strips)
- 1 onion (cut into half rings)
- 1 piece of ginger (approx. 2-4 cm, fresh, finely grated)
- 6 tbsp of sauce (sosu, yakisoba sauce)
- 4 tbsp of soy sauce (light japanese)
- 4 tbsp of sake
- 10g of bonito, dried flakes (katsuobushi)
- Algae, dried (aonori)
- 5 tbsp. Of oil (soybean oil or sunflower oil)
- Japanese mayonnaise

PREPARATION

Total time: approx. 30 minutes

1. Cook the pasta according to the package instructions, rinse thoroughly with ice-cold water and drain well.

2. Now let the oil get hot in a wok, in a pan or on a teppan (use a little oil on a teppan) and fry the meat and the prawns for about 3 minutes. Now fry the onion. As soon as the onion rings are glassy, add the ginger and carrots and fry for about 2 minutes, stirring constantly. Finally, fry the cabbage until it is tender.

3. Now add the drained pasta and fry for another 2 minutes. Be careful not to turn the pasta often, as they must be browned well, but do not let them burn. Now add the soy sauce and sake, and mix well. Finally, add the Sosu and stir together for another 4 minutes.

4. Arrange immediately on a platter, garnish with mayonnaise, sprinkle Aonori and Katsuobushi over it and serve.

UDON NOODLE SOUP

INGREDIENTS FOR 2 PORTIONS

- 4 packs of noodles (udon noodles)
- ½ surimi, japanese kamaboko
- 10g of spring onion (thin)
- 1.2 liters of dashi
- 4 tbsp of mirin
- 5 tbsp of soy sauce
- 0.4 tbsp of salt

PREPARATION

Total time: approx. 30 minutes

1. Cut the Kamaboko into approx. 5mm wide slices. Remove the roots of the spring onions and cut the spring onions diagonally into thin pieces.

2. Put the dashi in a saucepan and bring to a boil over medium heat. Add the mirin and soy sauce. Salt, bring to a boil again and then remove from the heat.

3. Fill a saucepan with water and bring the water to a boil. When the water boils, add the Udon noodles and cook with stirring (e.g. with chopsticks). After boiling the water again, pour the Udon noodles into a colander and let them drain.

4. Place the noodles in small bowls with the Kamaboko and spring onions. Pour over the broth

UDON NOODLES SOUP WITH CHICKEN

INGREDIENTS FOR 2 PORTIONS

- 175g of udon noodles, fresh
- 100g of chicken breast fillet without skin
- 2 pak choi (baby pak choi)
- 1 carrot
- 50g shiitake mushroom, fresh
- 1 shallot (peeled, finely diced)
- 1 clove of garlic, peeled, finely diced
- ¼ tbsp of ginger, fresh, peeled, finely diced
- Sesame oil, light
- 500ml of vegetable broth or chicken broth
- 1 tbsp of miso paste, light
- 1 spring onion
- Soy sauce (light)

PREPARATION

Total time: approx. 30 minutes

1. Cook the Udon noodles according to the package instructions, pour them into a sieve and let them drain. Cut the chicken into strips. Divide the pak choi, apart from the inside, into individual leaves, wash, and separate the green and white, possibly cut a little smaller. Peel the carrot, cut into julienne. Clean the shiitake mushrooms, remove the stems, cut the caps into slices. Clean and wash the spring onions and cut the white and green into rings separately.

2. Heat the oil in a saucepan; braise the shallot, the white Pak Choi and the spring onions and the garlic. Deglaze with the broth, add meat and shiitake, cook on low heat for five minutes. Mix the miso paste with a little hot broth in a small bowl, add to the saucepan, and do not let it boil. Add the Pak Choi greens, the carrot strips and the noodles, let them steep briefly, season with soy sauce and serve sprinkled with spring onion greens.

UDON NOODLES SOUP WITH SPINACH

INGREDIENTS FOR 2 PORTIONS

- 600ml of vegetable stock
- 2 shallots
- 2 cloves of garlic
- Ginger (fresh)
- 1½ tbsp of soy sauce
- 1½ tbsp of mirin
- 1 large carrot
- 150g of udon noodles, pre-cooked
- 100g of baby spinach
- 2 spring onions
- 1 shot of white wine vinegar
- 2 eggs (very fresh)

PREPARATION

Total time: approx. 30 minutes

1. Peel the shallots, ginger, and garlic, and dice finely. Let it soak in the broth with soy sauce and mirin over medium heat for three minutes. Peel the carrot, slice at an angle, add to the broth and cook for another three minutes.

2. Add the Udon noodles and cook according to the package instructions for about two minutes in the soup. Add the washed baby spinach and the cleaned and sliced spring onions shortly before the end of the cooking time. Drop the spinach together and season to taste.

3. At the same time, heat water in a saucepan with a dash of white wine vinegar. Beat the eggs one by one in a cup and carefully pour it into the hot water. Use a spoon to pull the egg whites around the yolk. Approximately poach for 3-4 minutes, lift out of the water and drain briefly. Serve in the soup.

UDON NOODLES WITH EGG AND SPRING ONIONS

INGREDIENTS FOR 1 PORTION

- 1 pack of udon noodles
- 1 egg
- 2 stems of spring onions

For the soup:

- 300ml of water
- 1½ tbsp of dashi, instant
- 1½ tbsp of soy sauce
- ½ tbsp of mirin
- 1 tbsp of sake

Extra:

- Pepper (japanese)
- Spice mix (togarashi)

PREPARATION

Total time: approx. 25 minutes

1. Wash the spring onions, cut them into bite-size pieces (approx. 2-3 cm) and mix with the whisked egg.

2. Put all ingredients for the soup in a saucepan and simmer on medium heat. If necessary, wash the Udon noodles, and add them to the boiling soup until they are ready.

3. Fry the prepared egg mixture in a pan. Serve the noodle soup and the finished egg mixture and sprinkle with pepper (preferably Japanese pepper) or Togarashi spice mixture if necessary.

UDON NOODLES WITH MUSHROOMS

INGREDIENTS FOR 4 PORTIONS

- 250g of noodles (udon)
- 2 tbsp of sunflower oil
- 1 onion (red, cut into rings)
- 1 toe of garlic (crushed)
- 450g of mixed mushrooms (e.g. Shiitake, oyster mushrooms, brown mushrooms)
- 350g of chinese cabbage (or pak choi)
- 2 tbsp of sherry (sweeter)
- 6 tbsp of soy sauce
- 4 spring onions (cut into rings)
- 1 tbsp of sesame seeds (toasted)

PREPARATION

Total time: approx. 30 minutes

1. Place the pasta in a large bowl and pour boiling water over them so that they are covered. Let it soak for 10 minutes or according to the package. Then drain thoroughly.

2. Heat sunflower oil in a large wok. Put the red onions and garlic in the wok and stir pan for 2-3 minutes. Add the mushrooms and continue stirring for about 5 minutes until cooked. Add Chinese cabbage or pak choi, noodles, sherry, and soy sauce to the wok. Mix all ingredients and stir pan for 2-3 minutes until the liquid boils.

3. Place pasta with mushrooms in preheated bowls and sprinkle with spring onions and toasted sesame.

UDON NOODLES PAN WITH TERIYAKI BUTTER

INGREDIENTS FOR 2 PORTIONS

- 200g of udon noodles
- For the sauce: "teriyaki butter sauce"
- 1 clove of garlic
- 1 pinch of thyme
- 75ml of teriyaki sauce
- 1 shot of soy sauce
- 1 teaspoon of honey
- 3 small pieces of butter (cold)
- For the vegetables:
- 1 pak choi
- 2 carrots
- 1 small zucchini
- 1 handful of sugar snaps
- 1 paprika
- 1 onion
- Oil for frying
- If possible; cashews
- Salt and pepper
- Sugar

PREPARATION

Total time: approx. 30 minutes

1. In the beginning, the teriyaki butter sauce can be prepared. To do this, put a little oil (I use coconut or peanut oil) in a small saucepan and press the garlic clove with a garlic press or cut it into small pieces and add it to the saucepan. Then sprinkle in the thyme and let it sauté briefly. Now pour everything with the teriyaki sauce and soy sauce and let it simmer.

2. The Udon noodles can be cooked at the same time.

3. Quarter the pak choi, peel the carrots and cut them into sticks. Wash the sugar snap peas well. Cut the bell pepper into strips and the zucchini into pencils. Halve the onion and then cut into rings.

4. Put oil in a pan. Briefly fry the pak choi, carrot sticks and sugar snap peas over high heat, season with salt, pepper, and sugar. Drain the Udon noodles and also briefly fry them. Reduce the heat and put the onions in the pan. Cover the pan with a lid and steam cook the contents of the pan for about 10 minutes. After 5 minutes add the peppers and zucchini.

5. In the meantime, turn off the hotplate of the saucepan and let the sauce cool down briefly. Then add 1 teaspoon honey and 3 small pieces of cold butter and stir. Let the sauce thicken for 2 minutes.

6. Now remove the lid from the pan and stir in the teriyaki butter sauce. Allow to pull through for 5 minutes over low heat.

7. Serve the dish with crushed cashew nuts

8. If you like meat in your meal, you can simply fry it in the pan at the beginning and leave it until the end.

UDON NOODLES WITH ASPARAGUS AND MUSHROOMS

INGREDIENTS FOR 2 PORTIONS

- 300g of udon noodles, pre-cooked
- 300g of asparagus, greener
- 150g of shiitake mushroom (fresh, alternatively mushrooms)
- 2 cloves of garlic
- Ginger
- 2 spring onions (lean)
- 2 tbsp of soy sauce
- 2 tbsp of rice vinegar
- Sugar, brown
- 1 tbsp of food starch
- Japanese spice mix (shichimi togarashi)
- Salt and pepper
- Oil

PREPARATION

Total time: approx. 30 minutes

1. Cook the Udon noodles in slightly boiling salted water for about two minutes, and drain it very well.

2. Wash asparagus, peel in the lower third, and cut into pieces. Clean the shiitake and cut into slices. Peel the cloves of garlic and ginger, dice very finely. Clean and wash the spring onions, cut the white and green into rings separately.

3. Mix the soy sauce, rice vinegar, sugar and cornstarch with 5 tablespoons of cold water.

4. Heat a little oil in a pan, fry the noodles briefly, then remove and set aside. Fry the shiitake; add the asparagus after about 3 minutes, then add garlic, ginger and the white of the spring onions and steam briefly. Add the pasta and the cornstarch mixture, bring to a boil once. Season with soy sauce, pepper, and Shichimi Togarashi and serve garnished with the spring onion green.

UDON NOODLES WITH MISO SAUCE

INGREDIENTS FOR 4 PORTIONS

- 600g of udon noodles (fresh or pre-cooked, alternatively spaghetti)
- 500g of ground beef
- 1 leek
- 3 spring onions
- 2 cloves of garlic
- ¼ cucumbers
- 250g of miso paste (50:50 light and dark, otherwise only dark)
- 80g of ginger
- 8 tbsp of soy sauce
- 200ml of sake
- 50 ml of mirin (alternatively sake or water)
- 3 tbsp of sugar
- Salt and pepper
- Oil for frying

PREPARATION

Total time: approx. 30 minutes

1. Wash the leek, shake well and dry, cut in half lengthways and cut into fine strips. You can also cut it first and then wash it in a colander under running water, this is easier. Then peel the ginger and cut as finely as possible. I usually make fine strips, but you can also grate it. Peel and finely chop the garlic. Combine these three ingredients.

2. Wash the spring onions too. Cut off the upper green part, and if desired, cut into rings. Cut the rest of the onions into thin strips. Wash the cucumber, cut in half and then cut into thin pieces, strips or quarters.

3. Put some oil in a pan or ideally a wok and heat briefly. As soon as the oil is warm, add the leek, garlic, and ginger, and then fry briefly until it starts to smell. Then add the minced meat and fry until crumbly. Season with a little pepper.

4. Mix the sake, mirin, miso paste, soy sauce, and sugar, and then pour over the chop and let it boil down until it thickens - this takes about 8-10 minutes.

5. Add the pasta and stir briefly again in the sauce. If you take packaged Udon noodles, simmer for about 2 minutes. If the pasta is already pre-cooked, heat it up briefly in the sauce.

6. Either sprinkle the cucumbers and spring onions on the plate or fold in just before you take it off the stove, then leave on the stove for a maximum of 1 minute so that the cucumber remains crisp.

UDON NOODLES WITH LEEKS AND SHRIMPS

INGREDIENTS FOR 4 PORTIONS

- 400g of noodles (udon), japanese
- Salt
- 4 liters of water
- 3 onions (diced)
- 250g of leek (cut into rings)
- 200g of carrot (grated)
- 50g of ginger root (grated)
- 100g of radish (grated)
- 4 tbsp of oil
- 250g of shrimp (uncooked, released)
- 4 tbsp of soy sauce
- 4 tbsp of sauce (sweet-sour), finished product
- 2 tbsp of sesame

PREPARATION

Total time: approx. 30 minutes

1. Cook the Udon noodles in 4 litre of salted water in about 8 minutes.

2. Heat the oil in a large pan; fry the onions, leek, carrots, and ginger in it for about 3 minutes. Drain the pasta. Mix with the prawns and the two sauces under the vegetables and cover. Let it simmer over low heat.

3. Roast the sesame seeds without fat in a pan and sprinkle them with the radish rasps over the pasta.

COLD UDON NOODLES WITH SOY SAUCE DIP

INGREDIENTS FOR 1 PORTION

- 1 pack of udon noodles, approx. 200 g
- 1 tbsp of soup spice (maggi)
- 1 tbsp of soy sauce
- 1 tbsp of dashi or vegetable broth
- 1 tbsp of mirin
- 1 piece of cucumber
- Lovage
- Tarragon
- Chili powder

PREPARATION

Total time: approx. 20 minutes

1. Place the Udon noodles in a microwave oven, pour a little water over them and let them cook for 3 minutes at 700 watts.

2. Stir in a cup of water, Maggi, soy sauce, dashi, and mirin - and add an ice cube if necessary to cool it.

3. Stir the Udon noodles until they are loose. Drain and quench with cold water until cool, then pour into cold or ice water.

4. Slice the cucumber. Place the Udon noodles on a plate and sprinkle with chili. Serve decorated with cucumber slices, tarragon, and lovage.

5. The dip can either be poured over the pasta or the pasta can be dipped.Add carrot, bamboo shoots, spring onions and everything your heart desires — as they will all go well with this.

FRIED UDON NOODLES WITH BEEF

INGREDIENTS FOR 1 PORTION

- 200g of udon noodles
- 130g of beef (cut into thin slices)
- 1 handful of bean sprouts
- 1 handful of chinese cabbage, cut into strips
- 5g of mu'er mushrooms (dried)
- 1 clove of garlic (chopped)
- 2 discs of ginger root (chopped)
- 1 shallot (finely chopped)
- 1 tbsp of oyster sauce
- Salt and pepper

PREPARATION

Total time: approx. 30 minutes

1. Pour boiling water over the Mu'er mushrooms, let them soak and cut into strips.

2. Pour boiling water over the Udon noodles and leave for 2-3 minutes. Let it brew until it's soft and you can get it apart.

3. In a little oil, briefly fry the chopped garlic and ginger together with the shallot and then add the thin strips of beef, fry very briefly, add the Mu'er mushrooms and season with a little salt. Afterwards, briefly fry the noodles and then add the Chinese cabbage, the soy sprouts, the soy sauce, the oyster sauce and 2-3 tablespoons of water, season to taste with salt and pepper and only continue to fry for a very short time.

NOODLES SOUP WITH CHICKEN

INGREDIENTS FOR 3 PORTIONS

- 1 liter of water (1 to 1 1/4 liter)
- 2 dice of broth
- 3 spring onions
- 2 large carrots
- 300g of chicken meat
- 3 pack of noodles (japanese instant noodles)
- Salt and pepper
- Curry
- Soy sauce
- 1 egg (boiled)

PREPARATION

Total time: approx. 25 minutes

1. Wash the spring onions, cut into thin slices. Peel the carrots, cut twice lengthways, then cut into thin (minimum approx. 5mm) triangles. Free the chicken from tendons and then cut into bite-size pieces.

2. Bring the water to a boil in a saucepan and dissolve the stock cubes in the water. Some stock cubes are more intense than others, so add as much to the water as it says on the package and then season. Cook the carrot corners until they're almost done.

3. Add the spring onions and the chicken, salt, pepper and add some curry. Taste again and again. You can season a little more because afterward the noodles are added, which take away some of the taste (or salt).

4. After the meat is cooked, add the pasta and cook. Then season again with soy sauce (I take about 4 sprinkles). When the pasta is done, season again and serve. If you like, you can also cut a boiled egg.

BAMI GORENG INDONESIAN NOODLES

INGREDIENTS FOR 3 PORTIONS

- 250 g of chinese egg noodles
- 1 leek
- 1 glass of bamboo shoot
- 1 large carrot
- 150g of cauliflower
- 1 glass of mushrooms (sliced or fresh)
- 200g of chicken fillet, fried, cut into pieces
- Soy sauce (wok sauce)
- Curry powder
- Soy sauce
- Soy sauce, japanese (teriyaki)
- Spice mix (chinese spice)
- Spice mix (tandoori masala)
- Cumin
- Ginger
- 1 tbsp. Of sauce (sweet-sour sauce)

PREPARATION

Total time: approx. 30 minutes

1. Prepare the pasta according to the package instructions.

2. Cut the leek into thick slices. Heat a dash of wok sauce in a pan and braise the leek in it. Quarter the carrot and cut into slices. Drain the bamboo shoots and add to the leek. Steam briefly, then mix in the carrot pieces, pour some wok sauce over them, season with curry, stir and let simmer for a few minutes. Cut the cauliflower into small florets, mix in and let everything simmer gently. Then drain the mushrooms, add them and let them heat up.

3. Drain the finished pasta, add immediately and chop a little. Next, mix in the pieces of meat and mix everything vigorously. Season with soy sauce, teriyaki sauce, sweet-sour sauce, and the spices, and stir again.

CHINA NOODLES

INGREDIENTS FOR 2 PORTIONS

- 250g of chinese egg noodles
- 1 bar of leek
- 1 bell pepper (red)
- 1 handful of bean sprouts, fresh
- 200g of chicken breast
- Soy sauce (dark, japanese)
- 200ml of chicken broth
- Pepper
- Spice mix (chinese spice)
- Oil

PREPARATION

Total time: approx. 25 minutes

1. Cook, pour and set aside the pasta according to the package instructions. Cut the leeks and peppers into pieces that are not too large. Do not dice the chicken breasts too large either. Approximately prepare 200ml of chicken broth.

2. Heat a wok or large pan. Add neutral oil. Now sear the meat vigorously in portions, season properly with salt and pepper, remove from the pan and keep warm. Then put the vegetables in the pan and fry with some color. Then add the meat again, as well as the drained, not too soft-cooked pasta. Add a lot of soy sauce (you should try your taste).

3. To keep the Asia pan nice and moist, deglaze with chicken broth so that the soy sauce can nestle nicely around the pasta. Season with a little Chinese spice and pepper. If the whole thing is too neutral, add more soy sauce. Do not worry; it will not be too salty since salt has been omitted overall.

NOODLES WITH EGG

INGREDIENTS FOR 1 PORTION

- 1 pack of pasta (noodles, of your choice)
- 1 egg
- 1 spring onion
- ½ carrot
- 1 shot of soy sauce
- 1 tbsp of sesame oil
- 1 tbsp of chili sauce (sweet, at will)
- ½ clove of garlic (at will)
- 1 tbsp of fried onions (alternatively peanuts or roasted sesame)
- Sambal oelek (at will)

PREPARATION

Total time: approx. 20 minutes

1. Cook the pasta in a small saucepan as shown on the package instructions. Keep about 1 or 2 tablespoons of the ramen broth, drain the pasta and pour the remaining broth away.

2. Wash the carrots and spring onions, cut the carrots into the finest possible sticks (e.g. you can peel them into thin slices with a vegetable peeler, then cut them into small strips), cut the spring onions into small slices. If you like, you can chop the garlic finely. Put the drained pasta back in a saucepan, add the onion, carrot and possibly garlic, and then mix well.

3. In a small bowl, whisk together the egg with the soy sauce, the cooled broth, (and if you like) sweet chili sauce and Sambal Oelek, and mix the egg mixture thoroughly with the pasta so that all the pasta are covered with egg. If the egg stops a bit, it is not a problem.

4. Add soybean oil in a pan and sauté the egg and noodle mixture in it until the egg is stocked everywhere, but not too dry. Sprinkle with the roasted onions, peanuts or sesame seeds and serve.

NOODLES SOUP WITH SAUERKRAUT

INGREDIENTS FOR 6 PORTIONS

- 450g of noodles
- 500g of sauerkraut
- 400g of pork neck (cut into short thin strips)
- 3 large ones of tomatoes
- 3 liters of vegetable stock
- 1 toe of garlic
- 1 tbsp of heaped sugar
- 3 tbsp of soy sauce
- 1 tbsp of sesame oil
- 2 tbsp of fish sauce
- 3 tbsp of tomato paste
- 1 tbsp of paprika
- 2 tbsp of heaped flour
- 1 tbsp of heaped five-spice powder
- 1 tbsp of heaped ginger
- 1 pinch of chili flakes
- Salt
- Oil (neutral)

PREPARATION

Total time: approx. 30 minutes

1. Peel the onion and cut it into large pieces, chop or press the garlic. Mix the finely chopped meat with flour, and dice the tomatoes.

2. Cook the pasta with one minute less cooking time.

3. Fry the meat in a high pan with neutral-tasting vegetable oil for about 3 minutes and then remove from the pan. Sauté onions with garlic until lightly browned. Add the sauerkraut and fry for 5 minutes.

4. Add all the spices. Put the pasta and broth in the pan (if you take instant broth, you can take the pasta water). Add the tomatoes and the meat and let everything simmer for 2 to 3 minutes, season to taste, then serve immediately.

JAPANESE FRIED NOODLE WITH MINCED MEAT

INGREDIENTS FOR 4 PORTIONS

- 500g of minced meat (mixed or beef)
- 300g of noodles (soba or mie noodles or spaghetti)
- Saltwater
- 1 piece of ginger (fresher)
- 2 cloves of garlic (fresh)
- 1 chili pepper, fresh
- 2 spring onions
- 50ml of soy sauce (japanese)
- 50ml of sake
- 1 tbsp of sesame oil
- Salt and pepper
- 2 tbsp of rapeseed oil

PREPARATION

Total time: approx. 30 minutes

1. Peel and grate the ginger (so you have no tough fibers). Chop the garlic finely (fresher does not leave such a strong stench, but a lot of aromas) and the chili (this is important to me), and then put aside. Wash, clean and cut the spring onions into fine rings and also set them aside.

2. Loosen the minced meat in a bowl and spread 3 tablespoons of soy sauce, 3 tablespoons of sake and 1 tablespoon sesame oil over the meat. Season with pepper, mix thoroughly and leave for 15 min. to let go.

3. During this time, let some noodles soak in salted water, pour off shortly before the end of the specified cooking time (collect 3 - 4 tbsp. of pasta water). Quench with cold water to complete the cooking process.

4. Let the rapeseed oil (or another neutral oil) heat up in a wok or high pan. Briefly fry the ginger, chili, and garlic so that the flavors get through, then reduce the heat a bit and fry the minced meat. Spread the meat finely and crumbly. Try some minced meat, add soy sauce if necessary.

5. When the meat is crispy, add the remaining sake and let the alcohol evaporate. Then add the pasta with the pasta water, swirl everything (or mix with tongs). Fry for 3-4 minutes. Season to taste with salt. Arrange in a pretty bowl and sprinkle the spring onions over it.

SPICY NOODLES WITH CHICKEN

INGREDIENTS FOR 4 PORTIONS

- 300g noodles
- 1 leek
- 1 eggplant
- 6 mushrooms
- 1 small dose of corn
- 500ml of tomato happened
- 4 chicken breast fillet
- 2 tbsp of sauce (wok sauce)
- 50 ml of vegetable stock
- 1 tbsp of heaped sambal oelek
- 1 tbsp of curry powder
- 1 tbsp of rosemary
- 1 tbsp of spice mix (chinese spice)
- 2 tbsp of soy sauce (japanese teriyaki sauce)
- Oil

PREPARATION

Total time: approx. 25 minutes

1. Cook the pasta. Cut the meat into pieces, fry in a little oil and set aside.

2. Cut the leek into thick rings, quarter the eggplant, cut into coarse slices and halve them again if necessary. Drain the corn and cut the mushrooms into slices.

3. Heat the vegetables in the wok sauce and stir until they are brown. Deglaze with the vegetable broth and mix in the Sambal Oelek. Drain the pasta and mix in with the meat and the tomatoes. Heat, season with the spices and mix vigorously.

4. Finally, season with the teriyaki sauce, stir again and serve.

BUCKWHEAT NOODLES WITH VEGETABLES

INGREDIENTS FOR 4 PORTIONS

- 250g of noodles (soba noodles - japanese buckwheat noodles)
- 250g of potato, firm cooking
- ½ head savoy cabbage, small (approx. 300 g)
- 3 liters of vegetable stock
- 1 teaspoon of salt
- 12 sheets of sage
- 1 large onion
- 5 toes of garlic
- 60g of butter
- 4 tbsp of rapeseed oil
- 50g of parmesan cheese (grated)
- Salt and pepper

PREPARATION

Total time: approx. 30 minutes

1. Peel the potatoes and cut them into small cubes. Clean the savoy cabbage and cut it into fine strips. Heat the vegetable broth, cook potatoes and savoy cabbage on low temperature for 15-20 minutes.

2. In the meantime, chop the sage, cut the cloves of garlic into thin slices and finely dice the onion. Heat the butter and oil together and fry the onion, garlic, and sage in the mixture until golden.

3. Now add the pasta to the vegetables in the broth and let them cook at a high temperature until they are al dente as instructed. Then pour on a sieve.

4. To serve, alternately place the pasta and cheese on the plates and pour the sage butter over them. Finally, sprinkle with pepper.

SOBA ROLLS

INGREDIENTS FOR 1 PORTION

- 1 tbsp of oil
- 125g of tuna (sushi quality or tuna fillet)
- 100g of noodles (soba noodles) broken into pieces
- Water
- 1 spring onion (the green), cut into thin rings
- 1 tbsp of soy sauce (light)
- ½ tbsp of rice vinegar
- Wasabi powder
- 1 tbsp of ginger (pickled, finely chopped)
- 6 nori leaves (toasted)
- ½ cucumber (peeled, cut into fine strips)

PREPARATION

Total time: approx. 20 minutes

1. Heat the oil in a pan and fry the tuna fillet on all sides for 6 minutes until it is almost done. Cut into stripes.

2. Cook the soba in a saucepan with boiling water until bite-proof, drain and rinse under running cold water. Drain thoroughly. Mix the soba carefully with spring onion, soy sauce, rice vinegar, a little wasabi, and pickled ginger.

3. Divide the pasta into 6 equal portions. Place a nori sheet with the glossy side down on a sushi mat and spread 1 portion of the pasta mixture on the lower third. Put a sixth of the cucumber on top, put a layer of tuna on top.

4. To roll up, fold the mat upwards, starting with the ingredients at the end and turning in the nori edge while rolling. Pull the mat up and continue rolling with even, light pressure. Moisten the top edge of the sushi roll with water to seal it. Push back the ingredients sticking out on the sides. The edges may look unfinished.

5. Remove the roll from the mat and cut it into 4 equal pieces. Arrange the sushi on a plate with the cutouts facing down. Do the same with the remaining ingredients.

PASTA WITH SLICED PORK AND PEAS

INGREDIENTS FOR 2 PORTIONS

- 500g of pork
- 1 tbsp of soy sauce
- 1 tbsp of mirin (japanese rice wine)
- 1 handful of peas (frozen)
- 1 tbsp of rapeseed oil or sunflower oil
- Salt and pepper
- Garlic
- 200g of noodles

PREPARATION

Total time: approx. 25 minutes

1. First stir a soy sauce and mirin into a teriyaki sauce (ready-made one is also available) and cook the noodles.

2. Fry the sliced pork in the oil. When the meat is almost cooked, deglaze with the previously mixed sauce. You can also add a little salt, pepper, and garlic to taste.

3. Finally, add a handful of frozen peas and the poured pasta, and swirl everything in the pan again properly. When the peas and the noodles are hot, the pork chop is done.

JAPANESE LEEK PASTA

INGREDIENTS FOR 4 PORTIONS

- 500g of penne
- 2 leeks
- 500g of ground beef or mixed minced meat
- 6g of dashi
- 100ml of soy sauce
- 2 cloves of garlic
- 2 tbsp of sugar
- 2 tbsp of sake
- 3 tbsp of sesame

PREPARATION

Total time: approx. 30 minutes

1. For the noodles, heat a saucepan with water and add dashi, soy sauce, and sake (about half of the stated amount).

2. Now fry the minced meat in a second saucepan and add the leek, cut into rings about 1cm wide, and fry. After about 5 minutes, when the meat is cooked, press in the cloves of garlic, add soy sauce, sake, and sugar and let it simmer a little. Before adding the pasta to the seasoned water, add about three ladles from the brew to the meat. The sauce can be thickened with cornstarch.

3. When the pasta is al dente, drain the water and mix the pasta with the minced meat and leek mixture.

4. The sesame can either be added in this way or briefly browned in a pan and then mixed in. It is also good for decorating the meal.

JAPANESE BOLOGNESE

INGREDIENTS FOR 2 PORTIONS

- 400g of ground beef (alternatively soy mince)
- 2 cm of ginger root (fresh)
- 1 bunch of spring onions
- 1 toe of garlic
- 4 tbsp of miso
- 3 tbsp of soy sauce
- 100ml of mirin (alternatively sherry)
- 2 tbsp of dashi (powder)
- 1 tbsp of sugar
- 400g of pasta, (udon, fresh)
- ¼ cucumbers
- 2 tbsp of sesame (white and black)

PREPARATION

Total time: approx. 30 minutes

1. Peel and finely chop the ginger and clove of garlic. Cut the spring onions into fine rings and set aside a small portion for the garnish. Wash and core the cucumber and cut into very fine strips about 6 cm long.

2. Fry the spring onions, the ginger and the garlic in neutral oil in a wok until glassy, then add the ground beef. Continue frying until the meat is cooked. Now stir in the miso paste, the soy sauce, the mirin, the dashi powder, and the sugar and let everything simmer for about 5 minutes at low temperature.

3. In the meantime, cook Udon noodles according to the package instructions. Spread the cooked pasta in small bowls, put the minced meat sauce on top and garnish with cucumber strips, spring onion rings, and sesame.

JAPANESE SESAME CHICKEN

INGREDIENTS FOR 4 PORTIONS

- 500g of chicken breast fillet, in pieces
- 1 pepper (in narrow strips)
- 1 chili pepper (finely chopped)
- 2m. In size carrot (in narrow strips)
- 2 tbsp of pepper (szechuan pepper)
- 10 tbsp of sesame
- 2 cloves of garlic (finely chopped)
- 5 tbsp of soy sauce (sweet, ketjap manis, substitute normal soy sauce)
- 6 tbsp of sesame oil, toasted
- 400g of noodles
- Oil (peanut oil)

PREPARATION

Total time: approx. 20 minutes

1. Cook the pasta in a little salted water for 3-5 minutes, drain and set aside. Toast the sesame in a pan without oil, and then set aside.

2. Let the pieces of meat soak in a saucepan with plenty of lightly boiling saltwater.

3. Heat the peanut oil in a pan, add the peppers, carrots, garlic, and chili, and fry for 5 minutes, then add the sesame, Szechuan pepper, ketjap manis, the chicken and the sesame oil and stir for another 3 minutes. Possibly add a dash of water.

4. Arrange with the pasta.

FRIED JAPANESE EGGPLANT

INGREDIENTS FOR 2 PORTIONS

- 1 eggplant (japanese)
- 1 clove of garlic
- 2 tbsp of olive oil
- 1 handful of cocktail tomatoes (halved or quartered)
- 2 tbsp of ajvar
- ½ tbsp of thyme
- Salt and pepper from the mill
- 2 packs of pasta such as spaghetti, linguine, or rice
- Mushrooms (or zucchini or onion)

PREPARATION

Total time: approx. 25 minutes

1. Cut the eggplant into small slices, cut the large slices in half again. You can also use normal eggplant, but the Japanese eggplant is less tart than normal and takes a little less rest.

2. Place the eggplant pieces on a board, sprinkle with salt and let the liquid soak for 5 minutes. In the meantime, prepare a bowl of oil, halve the cloves of garlic and press into the oil with a fork. Now season with a little salt, ground pepper, and add thyme and mix.

3. As soon as the eggplants have formed liquid on the surface, dab with a kitchen towel, then pour into the flavored oil. Mix well, then put on the pasta or rice as usual and cut the cocktail tomatoes.

4. Then heat a coated pan over medium heat. No additional oil is needed since the eggplant is already in place. Fry the eggplant, if you don't like it, take out the garlic. Then add the cocktail tomatoes and mix in the Ajvar. If necessary, add a small dash of water if it should be more liquid.

5. Drain the pasta or rice and serve everything together.

6. The recipe can be easily expanded with other ingredients that are still in the house. Mushrooms and zucchini, for example, also taste great in the spicy oil. A little parmesan goes well with this meal.

CHINESE CABBAGE SALAD

INGREDIENTS FOR 6 PORTIONS

- 1 chinese cabbage
- 1 bunch of spring onions
- 3 packs of ramen noodles
- 100g of almond, planed
- 50g butter
- 1 cup of sugar
- ¾ cup of oil
- ½ cup of soy sauce
- ½ cup of vinegar (5-herb vinegar)
- 1 bell pepper (red, as desired)

PREPARATION

Total time: approx. 30 minutes

1. Cut the Chinese cabbage into fine strips, cut the onions with green into slices.

2. Chop the ramen noodles with a hammer. Sauté together with the almonds in the hot butter until everything is golden brown. Let it cool down.

3. Make a dressing from sugar, oil, soy sauce, and vinegar. Shake well. Now mix all the ingredients well and let it steep for another 15 minutes.

4. If you still need some color for this salad, you can add a finely chopped red pepper.

CARBONARA

INGREDIENTS FOR 1 PORTION

- 1 egg
- 1 egg yolk
- 30g parmesan
- 2 discs of bacon
- 200 g of pasta (spaghetti)
- 2 tbsp of olive oil
- Salt and pepper

PREPARATION

Total time: approx. 30 minutes

1. Put egg, egg yolk, parmesan and pepper in a small bowl to taste. Whisk well with a fork.

2. Cut the bacon slices crosswise into strips about 1.5 cm wide. Fry in a pan, but it shouldn't be made crispy yet.

3. Cook the pasta according to the package instructions in boiling salted water.

4. Put the olive oil in the pan with the bacon, heat, and stir. As soon as the oil is hot, remove the pan from the heat. Pour some pasta water into the bacon and stir. Add the ramen noodles and mix. Add the egg mixture. Make sure that you put them on the pasta and not directly on the pan. Stir vigorously.

5. The heat from the pan turns the egg mixture into a creamy sauce. But if the eggs get too hot, it becomes a kind of scrambled eggs. If necessary, additional pasta water can be added to obtain a smooth but creamy sauce.

6. Serve sprinkled with parmesan and pepper.

JAPANESE STEW

INGREDIENTS FOR 4 PORTIONS

- 500g of minced
- 500g of pasta
- 500g of leek
- 750ml of broth

PREPARATION

Total time: approx. 15 minutes

1. Fry the chopped tomato paste and bring to a boil with the broth. Then add the spaghetti and leek and simmer for half an hour.

SPAGHETTI NAPOLI IN JAPANESE

INGREDIENTS FOR 2 PORTIONS

- 200g of spaghetti
- 3 small sausages (smoked)
- ½ onions
- ¼ bell pepper (green)
- 1 tbsp of oil
- 4 tbsp of ketchup
- Salt and pepper
- 50g of parmesan cheese (greaves)
- Parsley

PREPARATION

Total time: approx. 20 minutes

1. Cook the spaghetti with a little salt in a saucepan according to the package.
2. Cut the sausages into bite-size pieces. Cut the peppers and onions into thin strips.
3. Heat a large pan with the oil and fry the sausages, peppers, and onions in it for 1-2 minutes. Now add the cooked spaghetti and fry briefly, and then add the ketchup and season with salt and pepper.
4. Arrange the pasta with parmesan and parsley.

RAMEN BURGER

INGREDIENTS FOR 2 PORTIONS

- 400g of ramen noodles, alternatively mie noodles
- 2 beef burger patties
- 1 egg
- 1 shot of teriyaki sauce
- Arugula
- Spring onions
- Oil

PREPARATION

Total time: approx. 30 minutes

1. Prepare the pasta according to the package and let it cool.
2. Then mix with the egg. Heat the oil in the pan, add four palm-sized noodles to the pan and twist. Fry on both sides until golden brown. Then drain on kitchen paper.
3. Now you can prove it: First place the rocket and meat patty on one half of the pasta burger. Then drizzle with teriyaki sauce and top with spring onions cut into rings. Finish with the second half of pasta.

MEDIUM – 30/90 MINUTES

TRADITIONAL NOODLES SOUP

INGREDIENTS FOR 4 PORTIONS

- 600g of chinese egg noodles, thin
- 500g of pork loin
- 4 eggs (boiled, peeled)
- Bamboo shoot
- Sunflower oil or other vegetable oil
- Water
- 1 spring onion (cut into rings)
- 3cm of ginger, freshly peeled and grated
- 100ml of soy sauce
- 50ml of sake
- 1 tbsp of sugar
- 2 liters of water
- 4 tbsp of chicken broth (instant)
- 4 tbsp of soy sauce

PREPARATION

Total time: approx. 1 hour 30 minutes

1. The meat broth is prepared first. It is best to make them yourself.

2. Heat the sunflower oil in a saucepan and fry the loin (or alternatively lean pork) in it. Add the spring onions, ginger, soy sauce, sake, and sugar and fill with water so that the meat is covered. Now bring everything to a boil, switch it down and let it simmer for about 40 minutes. When the broth is half cooked, add the eggs. So they can take on the color with the meat. After cooking, the meat is cut into small pieces and the eggs cut in half.

Now for the main course:

1. Bring the 2 liters of water to a boil; add the instant chicken broth, the previously prepared meat broth (approx. 100ml) and the soy sauce. Let it simmer on a low flame.

2. Prepare the pasta separately and put them in the serving bowls or plates. Put the soup and eggs on top. Season with salt and pepper, garnish with fresh spring onions and enjoy.

3. The deposits can also vary depending on the season. For example, people like to add bamboo shoots in spring and mushrooms in autumn.

SOBA WITH MISO SOUP, MUSHROOMS AND BROCCOLI

INGREDIENTS FOR 2 PORTIONS

- 150g of soba noodles
- 1 liter of water (warm)
- 4 tbsp of miso paste (dark)
- 4 tbsp of soy sauce
- 2 tbsp of rice wine vinegar
- 1 tbsp of sesame oil
- 250g of mushrooms (brown)
- 5 spring onions
- 2 cloves of garlic
- 1 broccoli
- 2 tbsp of ginger
- 1 tbsp of chili flakes

PREPARATION

Total time: approx. 40 minutes

1. Slice the mushrooms. Cut the broccoli into florets. Slice the spring onions and set the green part aside. Chop the garlic finely.

2. First, cook the soba noodles in a large saucepan for 3 minutes and then pour into a colander and rinse cold.

3. Dry the pot and put it on the stove again. Put some oil in the saucepan and heat. Fry the mushrooms for about 5 minutes and lightly salt them. After 5 minutes, stir in the white part of the spring onions, garlic, and the ginger, then briefly sauté. Dissolve the miso paste in warm water and add the mixture together with the broccoli to the saucepan. Simmer the soup for 10-15 minutes until the broccoli is cooked. Finally, stir in soy sauce, rice wine vinegar, and sesame oil.

4. Spread the pasta on 2 bowls and spread the soup on top. Garnish the soup with the green part of the spring onions and the chili flakes.

NOODLES SOUP WITH PRAWNS

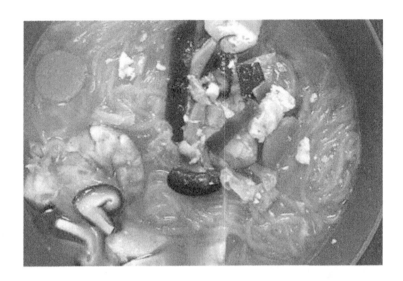

INGREDIENTS FOR 4 PORTIONS

- 100g of glass noodles
- 8 shiitake mushrooms
- 250g of cod fillet
- 12 king prawns
- 250g of tofu
- 2 carrots (thin)
- ½ head of chinese cabbage (approx. 250 g)
- 2 spring onions
- 1,000 ml of chicken broth (instant)
- 2 tbsp of sherry (dry)
- 3 tbsp of soy sauce
- 1 tbsp of lemon juice
- Cayenne pepper

PREPARATION

Total time: approx. 40 minutes

1. Cut the glass noodles into 10cm pieces, scald them with boiling water and let them steep for 2 minutes, then drain.

2. Clean the mushrooms and cut lengthways into quarters. Rinse fish fillet briefly, pat dry and cut into bite-size pieces. Remove the shell from the shrimp, leave the tailpieces on and gut them.

3. Cut the drained tofu into 8 cubes. Peel the carrots and slice them into thin slices. Clean, wash, halve and cut Chinese cabbage into strips of about 3cm wide. Clean the spring onions and slice them into thin slices.

4. Bring the broth to a boil. Add all the ingredients except the onions and let cook for 2 minutes. Finally, season with sherry, soy sauce, lemon juice, and cayenne pepper and sprinkle with the spring onions.

KIMCHI NOODLES SOUP

INGREDIENTS FOR 3 PORTIONS

- 350g of white cabbage
- 350g of red cabbage
- 1 leek
- 2 carrots
- 1 zucchini
- 2 cloves of garlic
- 1 piece of ginger root (approx. 3 cm)
- 1 large onion
- 1 glass of kimchi (approx. 400 g)
- 200g of tofu (japanese, fried)
- 2 tbsp of coconut oil
- 2 tbsp of palm oil (red)
- 100g of peas, frozen
- 800ml of vegetable stock (asian)
- 4 tbsp of soy sauce
- 2 tbsp of soy paste
- 2 spring onions
- 2 tbsp of chili flakes
- 150g of ramen noodles
- Sea-salt

PREPARATION

Total time: approx. 1 hour 15 minutes

1. Clean the cabbage and leek, and cut into strips. Clean zucchini and cut into cubes. Peel and slice carrots. Peel and chop the ginger, onion, and garlic.

2. Thaw frozen peas. Dice Japanese tofu. Heat palm and coconut oil in a saucepan. Braise the ginger, garlic, tofu cubes, and onions. Add the remaining vegetables and braise for another 5 minutes. Sprinkle with the sugar and let caramelize for 1 minute while stirring. Deglaze with the stock and add the Kimchi. Stir in soy sauce and soy paste. Season with the chili flakes. Bring everything to a boil and simmer on a low flame for 45 minutes.

3. Cut the spring onions into thin rings. Prepare the ramen noodles according to the package insert.

4. Place a portion of ramen noodles in a bowl and fill with the soup. Sprinkle with spring onions and serve.

UDON SOUP WITH MINCED MEAT

INGREDIENTS FOR 4 PORTIONS

- 500g of ground beef
- 4 packs of udon noodles (fresh)
- 1 zucchini
- 1 eggplant
- 1 bag of beans (green)
- 7 sheets of savoy
- 1 piece of pak choi
- 3 tbsp of thai curry paste, green
- 4 tbsp of sesame (white)
- 1 can of coconut milk (400 ml)
- Soy sauce
- Chili oil
- Sesame oil
- Salt and pepper

PREPARATION

Total time: approx. 1 hour

1. Slice the eggplant and quarter it. Cut the zucchini and savoy cabbage into strips. Roast the sesame dry in a coated pan, remove and set aside.

2. Fry the eggplant slices in sesame oil in a deep pan until they become a little soft. Add zucchini, savoy cabbage, and beans and continue to fry for about 5 minutes.

3. It is best to sear the ground beef in parallel in a second pan. Crush the sesame seeds with 3 teaspoons of curry paste and mix with the ground beef. Add the ground beef to the vegetables in the deep pan and mix well. Add 1 liter of beef broth and let it boil down. Season with salt and pepper. If you like, you can add a hint of soy sauce and chili oil.

4. Only add the coconut milk at the end. Let it steep briefly on medium heat. Cook the Udon noodles in parallel.

5. Arrange everything in a deep plate or bowl. Garnish with pak choi.

UDON SOUP WITH CURRY

INGREDIENTS FOR 3 PORTIONS

- 1 pack of noodles (udon)
- Oil
- 1 bunch of spring onions
- 1 onion
- 1 carrot
- 400g of chicken breast fillet or turkey breast fillet
- 2 tbsp of soy sauce
- 500ml of water (possibly more)
- Dashi
- Curry paste
- 1 tbsp of food starch

PREPARATION

Total time: approx. 40 minutes

1. First, cut the meat into bite-size pieces and put it in a little soy sauce. Clean the spring onions and cut them into rings. Peel and dice the onion and cut the carrots into thin slices.

2. Put a little oil in a wok and first sauté the onions, spring onions and carrots. Then add the pickled meat and fry until the meat is cooked. In addition, prepare the pasta according to the package instructions.

3. Deglaze the contents of the wok with the 2 tbsp. of soy sauce. Add water and dashi. The packaging shows how much dashi belongs in which amount of water, this varies from product to product.

4. Add the curry paste when everything is boiling and dissolve. If the soup is too thin despite the curry paste, simply thicken it with cornstarch. Add the pasta to the soup and serve.

5. Tip: Do not take the round moist Udon noodles, but the dried ones.

UDON NOODLES SOUP WITH PORK FILLET

INGREDIENTS FOR 2 PORTIONS

- 750ml of chicken broth (homemade, not an instant)
- 10g dashi (dashi powder, from the asian shop corresponds to 1 small bag)
- Pork
- 2 fret of spring onion (less depending on size)
- 2 eggs (hard-boiled)
- 2 pack of udon noodles (200 g each, fresh)
- Salt and pepper
- Soy sauce

PREPARATION

Total time: approx. 1 hour

1. Parry the pork fillet, if necessary fold in the flat end a little and tie it together using a kitchen thread so that it does not dry out when seared and in the oven. The fillet is only peppered and salted when it comes out of the oven.

2. Put the fillet in a hot pan and sear well for about 8-10 minutes.

3. Meanwhile preheat the oven to 100 degrees top and bottom heat.

4. Remove the pork fillet from the pan, wrap it in a piece of aluminum foil and put it in the oven for 30 minutes.

5. Boil the pasta in a saucepan according to the package instructions. Drain and quench with cold water, and then spread over two large bowls.

6. Put the chicken broth in a saucepan, mix with the dashi powder and heat. Meanwhile, clean the spring onions and cut them into small rings. Peel the eggs and split them in the middle.

7. After 30 minutes, take the pork fillet out of the oven, add pepper and salt, and then cut into slices about 1cm thick. The juice in the aluminum foil can of course also be added to the broth.

8. Add the soup to the noodles in the two bowls. Then drape the slices of pork fillet along the edge, place 2 egg halves in a bowl and divide the spring onions cut into rings between the two bowls.

9. If you want, you can fry the leek with a little chili instead of the spring onions, deglaze with soy sauce and add to the soup.

10. The recipe is very variable; you can let off steam when it comes to the composition of the soup.

11. The portion is really huge and can be adjusted according to hunger. If there are leftovers from the pork fillet, they can be eaten cold the next day.

UDON SOUP WITH CHICKEN

INGREDIENTS FOR 4 PORTIONS

- 400g of udon noodles
- 200g of chicken fillet
- Soy sauce
- 1 shot of sake
- 1 carrot
- 6 shiitake mushroom or similar
- 1,150ml of dashi or other broth
- 100g of spinach
- 2 spring onions
- 3 tbsp of mirin
- 4 eggs

PREPARATION

Total time: approx. 1 hour

1. The preparation takes a little time – so you have to be fast with it.

2. Bring 1.5 liters of water to a boil and let the noodles cook for 10 minutes. Take care that it does not foam. Add a little cold water if necessary and stir from time to time so that the pasta does not stick together. Place the pasta in a colander and cold-chill.

3. Cut the chicken into bite-size pieces and marinate with a good dash of soy sauce and sake for ten minutes.

4. Peel and slice the carrot. Clean the mushrooms and cut them into slices about 0.5cm thick. Wash and select spinach. Cut the spring onions into pieces approx. 2.5cm long.

5. Depending on the firmness or cooking time, gradually add the ingredients to the 1,150ml broth with mirin. First, add the carrot slices. After about two minutes, add the chicken, and after another two minutes, add the mushrooms (if you want to add pak choi or something else, add these ingredients accordingly). Then season with mirin, soy sauce, and pepper.

6. Now the noodles come in portions in four soup bowls. Spread a few leaves of spinach on top and put the soup on top.

7. Preheat the oven to 200°C top/bottom heat.

8. Slide one egg each into a soup bowl and place the ready-to-serve dishes in the oven for about ten minutes until the egg is ripe.

9. Serve the soup bowls from the oven directly with chopsticks. And remember: in Japan, you can sip while eating soup.

10. Tips: You can still vary the ingredients for the stew. If you like, you can also add Japanese eggplant or Pak Choi.

UDON NOODLES WITH PEANUTS AND VEGETABLES

INGREDIENTS FOR 4 PORTIONS

- 400g of udon noodles (fresh)
- 400g carrot
- 250g mushrooms
- 2 fret of spring onions
- Chili pepper
- 100g of peanuts (roasted and salted)
- 1 piece of ginger
- 2 toes of garlic
- 75ml of mirin
- 150ml of sake
- 200ml of beef broth or vegetable broth
- 50ml of soy sauce, preferably japanese
- Five-spice powder
- Honey
- Pepper
- Gravy

PREPARATION

Total time: approx. 50 minutes

1. Peel and finely chop the ginger and garlic. Cut the chili into fine rings. Peel the carrots and cut them into fine strips or rings. Clean the mushrooms, remove the stems and quarter them. Clean the spring onions and cut them into rings.

2. Briefly fry ginger and garlic in a little oil, then deglaze with beef or vegetable stock, sake, soy sauce, and mirin. The quantities given for the liquids are only approximate values. The amount and composition can vary depending on the taste and sauce requirements, so maybe not at the beginning; do not pour the complete amount of liquid into the pot, but gradually do it if necessary.

3. Add carrots and chilies, and simmer for five minutes, then add the mushrooms and spring onions and simmer for another 3-5 minutes. Season with the five-spice powder and possibly honey and pepper, and if necessary, thicken with sauce binders, depending on how much sauce you have made and how thick you want this sauce to be. Finally, stir the Udon noodles and let them steep for approx. 2-5 minutes, so that they get warm and taste.

4. Serve with the roasted peanuts.

UDON NOODLES WITH TOFU AND SPINACH IN PEPPER SAUCE

INGREDIENTS FOR 4 PORTIONS

- 2 handfuls of baby spinach
- 270g of udon noodles
- 200g of tofu
- 1 tbsp of sesame oil

For the sauce:

- 50ml of water
- 6 tbsp of soy sauce
- 3 tbsp of rice vinegar
- 2 tbsp of food starch
- 1 tbsp of pepper
- 3 tbsp of garlic
- 2 tbsp of agave nectar
- 1 tbsp of ginger powder

PREPARATION

Total time: approx. 40 minutes

1. For the pepper sauce, dissolve the starch in cold water. Add soy sauce, rice wine vinegar, ginger, agave syrup, garlic and pepper, and use in a blender to make a smooth sauce.

2. Bring the water to a boil and cook the noodles for 4-5 minutes until they are firm to the bite. Drain the pasta and rinse with cold water to prevent them from sticking together.

3. Cut the tofu into cubes. Heat some sesame oil in a larger pan and fry tofu until the cubes are brown all around. Remove the pan from the hob, deglaze with a dash of water, add a dash of pepper sauce and swirl the pan through once so that the tofu is glazed all around. Set the tofu aside.

4. Pour some sesame oil into the pan that has already been used. When the oil is hot, add the pasta and pepper sauce. Fry the noodles with constant stirring until they are completely covered with sauce. Remove the pan from the heat and stir in the spinach and tofu cubes.

5. Divide the pasta into 4 plates and serve garnished with sesame.

6. Tip: The amount of tofu and spinach can be varied as desired.

UDON NOODLES WITH PORK AND VEGETABLES

INGREDIENTS FOR 2 PORTIONS

- 2 pack of japanese noodles (udon, the fat ones)
- 2 small onion or 1 large one
- 1 zucchini
- 2 potatoes
- 2 toes of garlic
- 300g of pork belly or neck
- 2 tbsp. Of spice paste (black bean paste, heaped tablespoons)
- 2 tbsp. Of potato starch
- Mix water
- Vegetable oil
- 1 teaspoon of sesame oil
- 5 small mushrooms
- 200ml of beef broth or pork broth
- 200ml of water
- Extra: cucumber for garnish

PREPARATION

Total time: approx. 40 minutes

1. Cut the onion into eighths and separate the pieces. Cut the zucchini and mushrooms into small cubes, then (if you want, peeled) potatoes and the pork belly into 1-2 cm cubes. Cut or press the garlic very finely and mix the potato starch with a little water. Prepare the pasta according to the package instructions.

2. Fry the pork belly with a little oil in a wok or large pan for 4-5 minutes until crispy brown. If you want, you can soak up the pork fat with a kitchen towel.

3. Now add the potatoes, zucchini, onion, and the mushrooms and continue to heat for about 2 minutes. Stir well. Now push the meat and vegetables to the edge so that you have a free area in the middle.

4. Put 1 tablespoon of oil in this area, wait a little while until it is hot and add the black bean paste. Fry while stirring, turn down the heat, then stir in the vegetables and meat with the paste.

5. Now add the broth and 100-200ml of water and close the wok with a lid and leave it for 10-15 min. Simmer until the potatoes are done. Now carefully stir in the starch water and continue stirring until you have a thick sauce.

6. Spread the noodles in bowls; pour a lot of sauce over them. If necessary garnish with a little cucumber and enjoy.

UDON CHICKEN BREAST WITH

INGREDIENTS FOR 4 PORTIONS

- 600g of chicken breast
- 2 tbsp of sesame oil
- 150ml of sauce (teriyaki – in my recipe)
- 350g of noodles (udon)
- 2 tbsp of oil (peanut)
- 2 carrots
- 250g of beans (green, as narrow as possible - princess beans)
- 1 bunch of spring onion (the white, cut into fine cubes)
- 1 clove of garlic (cut into fine cubes)
- 1 tbsp of ginger root (grated)
- Salt and pepper
- 1 tbsp of cayenne pepper

PREPARATION

Total time approx. 45 minutes

1. Triple the data in my recipe for the Teriyaki sauce from the database and slowly reduce it to almost a third of the amount simmering to make the sauce very sticky.

2. Cut carrots and peppers into Julienne with a length of 5cm and cook crispy in peanut oil for 5 minutes. Then mix in the onion, a clove of garlic and the ginger, lightly salt it and leave it to stand for 5 minutes.

3. Blanch beans for 4 minutes, then halve in length and add to the vegetables with the cayenne pepper.

4. Now mix the bite-proof pasta with the vegetables and mix in half of the teriyaki reduction. Turn several times.

5. At the same time, platter the chicken breasts on the thicker side and roast to the point so that they are just through. Brush with the rest of the teriyaki sauce. Finally, lightly salt and pepper. Cut the breasts crosswise into slices and arrange the vegetable mix next to or above the noodle.

JAPANESE COLD BUCKWHEAT NOODLES WITH DIP

INGREDIENTS FOR 4 PORTIONS

- 600g of noodles (soba, japanese buckwheat noodles)
- 4 spring onions
- 1 nori sheets
- Wasabi paste (japanese, green, from a tube or powder)

For the sauce:

- 1½ cup of water
- 0.33 cup of sake, alternatively white wine or mild sherry
- 1 tbsp of sugar
- 0.33 cup of soy sauce (japanese)
- 0.33 tbsp of dashi (japanese instant fish broth)

PREPARATION

Total time approx. 50 minutes

1. Bring all ingredients for the sauce to a boil briefly, and then simmer for 2-3 minutes over low heat. Cool in a water bath and then refrigerate for at least 30 minutes.

2. Cut the spring onions into fine rings. If available, cut Nori into thin strips with scissors.

3. Boil soba in plenty of boiling water according to the package instructions, and then put in a colander and quench ice-cold. Rinse well, and then drain.

4. Place the pasta in 4 plates (sprinkle with Nori strips if necessary), distribute the sauce in 4 dip bowls.

5. Everyone mixes spring onions and wasabi (be careful, very spicy) in the dip sauce and dips the noodles (chopsticks-for-chopsticks or fork-for-fork) briefly into the sauce. A typical summer meal in Japan.

NOODLES WITH FRIED TOFU AND BROCCOLI

INGREDIENTS FOR 4 PORTIONS

- 200g of broccoli
- Sea-salt
- 200g ramen noodles
- 250g of tofu (japanese fried)
- 6 m in size of mushrooms
- 1 onion (red)
- 2 chili pepper (fresh)
- 1½ tbsp of bean paste, black
- ½ tbsp of five-spice powder
- 3 tbsp of soy sauce, dark
- 2 cloves of garlic
- Peanut oil
- Sesame oil
- 5 stems of coriander

PREPARATION

Total time: approx. 1 hour 15 minutes

1. Wash the broccoli, separate the florets and cut them into smaller pieces. Cook the broccoli bite-proof in sufficient saltwater over medium heat for 5-7 minutes. Then pour into a sieve, quench cold and let it drain.

2. Cook the ramen noodles according to the package instructions, pour them into a sieve and let them drain.

3. Cut the tofu into cubes. Clean the mushrooms and cut them into thick slices. Peel the red onion and cut lengthways into narrow slices. Halve, clean, core and chop the chilies. Mix the bean paste and five-spice powder with chilies, 2 tablespoons of soy sauce, and vegetable broth. Peel and press the garlic.

4. Heat sufficient peanut and sesame oil in a wok and fry the tofu all around, salt and remove from the wok. Pour in some oil, then briefly fry the mushrooms and onion while stirring. Add broccoli and stir briefly. Pour in the seasoning broth and mix everything. Cook on medium to high heat for 5 minutes, stirring, until the broth is almost completely boiled down.

5. Finally, add the ramen noodles and tofu and mix in, continue to stir until the sauce is almost completely absorbed by the ramen noodles and everything is well covered with it, season with the remaining soy sauce.

6. Decorate with coriander and serve.

YAKISOBA SALMON

INGREDIENTS FOR 4 PORTIONS

- 300g of noodles (japanese noodles of your choice, e.g. Soba)
- 300g of vegetables of your choice (e.g. B. Broccoli, zucchini, carrots, baby corn, pak choi, spinach)
- 2 spring onions
- 1 cloves of garlic
- Salt and pepper
- For the fish:
- 4 salmon fillets
- 2 tbsp of marinade (homemade of your choice, e.g. B. Based on soy sauce or lemon juice)
- Sesame (optional)

PREPARATION

Total time: approx. 40 minutes

1. Wash the salmon and dry it with kitchen paper.

2. Heat a pan with tasteless oil over medium heat, add the garlic until the garlic has flavored the oil, and then remove. Add the spring onion and the vegetables, and fry.

3. Cook the noodles in hot water a little shorter than indicated on the package.

4. The Japanese use soba noodles, but use whatever you want, but never use Italian pasta.

5. Put 1 1/2 tablespoons of the pasta water in the pan, this prevents the vegetables from burning, for example, and makes it cook a little faster. Then you put the noodles in the pan and the vegetables that don't need cooking, such as pak choi and spinach. Reduce the heat and season with salt and pepper.

6. Heat some oil in another pan. Fry the salmon on both sides. It should still be slightly glassy in the middle.

7. Drape the yakisoba on a plate and add the salmon as you like.

8. Brush the salmon with the marinade and sprinkle sesame seeds on top.

SALMON FILLET

INGREDIENTS FOR 2 PORTIONS

- 2 salmon fillets
- For the marinade:
- 1 lemon (the juice of it)
- 1 lime (the juice of it)
- 2 cloves of garlic
- Pepper (szechuan pepper and japanese mountain pepper, both lemon-heavy)
- 1 tbsp of rosemary
- 1 tbsp of thyme
- 5 tbsp of olive oil (preferably from crete)

For the vegetables: (ratatouille)

- 2 onions (finely diced)
- 1 clove of garlic (finely diced)
- 1 zucchini (finely diced)
- 1 pepper (red, finely diced)
- 4 tomatoes (finely diced)
- Salt
- Sugar
- 2 packs of tagliatelle
- Sea salt (maldon sea salt)

PREPARATION

Total time: approx. 40 minutes

1. For the marinade, combine the juice of the fruit, the Szechuan pepper and the remaining ingredients for the marinade and mix with the hand blender. Wash the salmon, pat dry and marinate in a freezer bag with the marinade for several hours (even better overnight) in the fridge.

2. Preheat the oven to 150 ° C.

3. Put on the water for the pasta. When it boils, give it plenty of salt (approx. 2-3 teaspoons) and cook the pasta 2-3 minutes less than stated on the package. Then don't be put off! Very important!

4. Now remove the salmon from the freezer bag and save the marinade. Place a piece of fish on the aluminum foil. Season with Japanese mountain pepper and a little salt and pour 2 teaspoons of the marinade on top, then close the foil tightly. Do the same with the second piece.

5. For the ratatouille, fry the onion and garlic cubes in olive oil in a pan, then remove from the pan. Then add the paprika and zucchini cubes, sweat in it and let it take a little color. Finally, add the tomato cubes and cook everything.

6. Put the fish in the aluminum foil on a rack for 10 minutes in the hot oven and cook.

7. Now season the vegetables with salt and sugar. Add the rest of the marinade to the vegetables and bring to a boil. Season everything well.

8. Drain the pasta and add to the vegetables, bring to a boil once and finish cooking in the vegetables for about 2-3 minutes.

9. Now serve the ratatouille pasta on a plate. Place the fish in the foil next to it - open the foil on the table a little, so you can smell the aroma vapor. Sprinkle with a little Maldon Sea Salt Flakes as desired. Serve immediately.

SHIRATAKI NOODLES WITH MINCED MEAT AND GINGER

INGREDIENTS FOR 1 PORTION

- 100g of ground pork
- 200g of shirataki noodles
- 1 onion
- 1 tbsp of sugar
- 1½ tbsp of soy sauce
- 1 tbsp of sake
- 1 small piece of ginger
- Oil

PREPARATION

Total time approx. 45 minutes

1. Cut the onion into thin slices.

2. Drain the Shirataki noodles, rinse and boil for about 3 minutes in hot salt water so that the slightly fishy smell disappears. Peel the ginger and cut it into fine cubes.

3. Heat some oil in a saucepan and fry the ginger in it. Then add the minced meat and fry gray. Deglaze with the sake. Add the onion and shirataki noodles. Stir well so that everything is covered with oil. Add the sugar and braise everything until the onions are translucent.

4. Finally, add the soy sauce and continue cooking until the shirataki noodles have accepted the taste well.

JAPANESE NOODLE SOUP WITH FRIED TOFU

INGREDIENTS FOR 2 PORTIONS

- 300g of tofu (natural, firm)
- 2 tbsp of soy sauce (japanese)
- 1 tbsp of mirin
- 2 tbsp of sake
- 4 tbsp of broth (e.g. Dashi)
- 100ml of oil (for deep frying)

For the soup:

- 600ml of broth (dashi), also vegetarian
- 250g of noodles (udon), thick wheat noodles
- 2 spring onions (the green parts)
- ½ tbsp of salt (as needed)
- Soy sauce

PREPARATION

Total time: approx. 1 hour

1. You can either buy the fried tofu ready or make it yourself. To make it yourself, you wrap the cube-shaped solid tofu with kitchen paper, weigh it down for a quarter of an hour with a chopping board or saucepan so that the liquid it contains is squeezed out. Then cut it into 3-4 mm thick square slices. The ingredients for the marinade are heated in a pan, the tofu slices are put in and the mixture is simmered over low heat until the liquid has evaporated. Carefully turn the slices once.

2. Now wipe the pan dry (or take a new one) and heat the oil, which should be about 1cm high. Three or four slices of tofu are always fried at once, turned once. When the slices have become a little brown, put them on kitchen paper to drain them. With another sheet of kitchen paper, which is placed over it, the excess oil is also removed from the top. The squares are cut into triangles (like fox ears).

3. For the soup, boil the noodles in lightly salted water for 2-3 minutes according to the instructions, briefly brew them in a pasta strainer with cold water and distribute them in two bowls. Add the hot dashi, a couple of tofu slices on top and finally, the green parts of the spring onions cut diagonally into fine rings.

OTSU SALAD

INGREDIENTS FOR 2 PORTION

- 340g soba noodles
- 340g of tofu (firm)
- 1 lemon (grated zest of it)
- 1 piece of ginger root (thumb-sized, peeled and grated)
- 1 tbsp of honey
- ¾ tbsp of cayenne pepper
- ¾ tbsp of sea salt
- 1 tbsp of lemon juice (fresh)
- 60ml of rice vinegar (unseasoned, brown)
- 80ml of soy sauce
- 2 tbsp of olive oil
- 2 tbsp of sesame oil (dark, from roasted sesame seeds)
- ½ bundle of coriander green (chopped)
- 3 spring onions (thinly sliced)
- ½ large cucumber or 1 small one (peeled, halved lengthways, cored, cut into thin slices)
- 1 handful of coriander green for garnish
- 4 tbsp of sesame seeds (toasted, for garnish)

PREPARATION

Total time: approx. 40 minutes

1. Cook the soba noodles in package directions. Then drain and rinse under cold water.

2. Heat a coated pan without fat and roast the sesame seeds until they take on color and spread a nutty scent.

3. Drain, dry, and dice the tofu, then fry in a pan with a lot of oil until crispy and golden brown.

4. Mix lemon zest, ginger, honey, cayenne pepper, and salt for the dressing until it has a mushy consistency. Add lemon juice, rice vinegar, and soy sauce. Finally, add the oils and always stir.

5. Mix the soba noodles, coriander, spring onions, cucumber, and a small part of the dressing in a large bowl. Finally, add the tofu and garnish with the remaining dressing, a few coriander leaves, and the toasted sesame seeds.

SOY STOREY

INGREDIENTS FOR 3 PORTIONS

- 200g of noodles (ramen, or mien noodles)
- 1 egg yolk (class m)
- 150g of baby spinach
- 1 clove of garlic
- 10g of ginger
- 7 tbsp of sunflower oil
- 1 tbsp of sesame oil
- 1 tbsp of honey
- 2 tbsp of soy sauce
- Salt and pepper
- Sugar
- 300g of ground beef
- 2 discs of cheese
- 6 tbsp of teriyaki sauce
- 3 tbsp of mayonnaise
- 1 tbsp of wasabi paste
- 1 mini-cucumber
- 1 tomato
- 2 spring onions

PREPARATION

Total time: approx. 1 hour

1. Cook the pasta in plenty of boiling salted water according to the package instructions. Scare the pasta cold, drain in a sieve and pat dry with kitchen paper. Whisk egg yolk and mix with the pasta in a bowl. Divide the pasta into 4 round molds of approx. 3cm high (diameter 8-10 cm). Cover with cling film, press firmly and - for example, weigh down with a can of tomatoes. Place in the fridge for 20-30 minutes.

2. In the meantime, wash spinach and spin dry. Peel and finely dice the ginger. Also dice the garlic finely. Heat 1 tablespoon of oil, sesame oil, and honey in a pan. Fry the garlic and ginger until golden yellow. Add the spinach and let it collapse. Season with soy sauce, pepper, salt, and 1 pinch of sugar and set aside.

3. Knead the meat with 2 tbsp. of teriyaki sauce and season well with pepper. Form 2 patties from the mass. Mix the mayonnaise and wasabi paste. Cut the cucumber into slices. Slice the tomato. Clean, wash and cut the spring onions into thin strips.

4. Remove the pasta from the molds. Heat 4 tablespoons of oil in a coated pan and fry the pressed noodles on each side for 5-6 minutes. Then drain on kitchen paper and keep warm in the oven.

5. Heat the remaining oil in a pan. Season the patties with salt and pepper and fry on each side for 3-4 minutes. After turning, deglaze with the remaining teriyaki sauce and pour the cheese onto the patties.

6. Place 1 packet of pasta with tomato, cucumber, spring onions, drained spinach, and patties. Drizzle with the mayonnaise and finish with the remaining noodle packages

GRILL OR BAKE RAMEN PIZZA

INGREDIENTS FOR 2 PORTIONS

- 200g of ramen noodles, dried
- 2 eggs
- 1 tbsp of sunflower oil
- 250ml of tomatoes (happened)
- 2 tbsp of herbs of Provence

For covering:

- Salami, ham, mushrooms, onions, and olives, etc.
- 300g of gouda (grated)

PREPARATION

Total time: approx. 50 minutes

1. Put ramen in hot water and soak for three minutes. Drain the water and let the ramen cool. Then mix the two whisked eggs into the ramen.

2. Coat the baking sheet with oil. Layout a thin layer of ramen. Sprinkle a fine layer of cheese on top. Sprinkle the sieved tomatoes over it. Sprinkle with herbs from Provence. Now pour a little cheese over it again.

3. Garnish with a topping (your choice).

4. Bake in the grill at around 350°C until the bottom becomes crispy (can take between 8-15 minutes).

Note:

- The recipe is of course also successful in the oven - it takes a little longer (approx. 200 degrees). Some even fry the ramen pizza in the pan.

MISO RAMEN WITH SMOKED TERIYAKI

INGREDIENTS FOR 2 PORTIONS

For the broth:

- 500ml of water
- 250ml of meat soup
- 2 large oranges
- 3 tbsp of soy sauce (light)
- 3 tbsp of oyster sauce
- 2 tbsp of honey
- 1 tbsp of ginger (grated)
- 1 thai chili
- 2 discs of smoked bacon (intense, no black forest ham)
- 2 nori sheets
- 3 tbsp of miso paste
- 2 cloves of garlic
- 1 tbsp of apple cider vinegar (or rice vinegar)

For the meat:

- 400g of meat (as you like; chicken, beef, shrimp, etc.)
- 1 clove of garlic
- 3 tbsp of soy sauce
- 1 tbsp of honey
- 1 large orange
- 1 tbsp of ginger (grated)

Moreover:

- 2 pack of ramen noodles
- For the vegetables:
- 1 small federation of spring onion (fresh)
- 1 bag of bean sprouts, fresh
- 1 bowl of mushrooms (fresh, shiitake mushrooms)
- 50g of carrot (grated)
- 50g of celery (grated)

PREPARATION

Total time: approx. 1 hour 25 minutes

For the broth:

1. Bring the water and broth to a simmer. Strip the orange peel away from the oranges. Squeeze the oranges and pour the juice into the boiling broth. Add the soy sauce, oyster sauce, honey, ginger, chili pepper, smoked bacon, nori leaves, miso paste, and 2 pressed cloves of garlic and simmer gently for 45 minutes. Season the broth to taste.

2. Parry the meat.

3. Let the broth simmer for another 10 minutes. The broth should taste very strongly sweet-salty-smoky towards the end and almost 1/3 of the actual liquid should have evaporated. Add the vinegar. Then briefly boil the broth and set aside. Season the broth again as it is important that it is very intense. You can continue to taste and add soy sauce, miso paste, and honey. If too much liquid has escaped, add water.

For the meat:

1. Cut the meat into bite-size pieces and cook in the soup for 5 minutes as soon as the soup has boiled down for at least 30 minutes. Then remove the meat again.

2. In a pan, for a marinade; add honey, soy sauce, grated ginger, pressed cloves of garlic, and boil the orange strips of the orange and its juice until a very flavorful syrup is obtained. Briefly turn the cooked meat in it and set aside for marinating.

3. According to the instructions, cook the ramen noodles. It is important not to add salt.

For the vegetables:

1. Wash everything and cut into pieces or strips as desired. Wash and set the bean sprouts aside. The spring onions, mushrooms, carrots, and celery are just suggestions. You can also add other vegetables here. Pak choi or sugar snap peas and other crunchy vegetables are particularly suitable. Please make sure that you can eat the corresponding vegetables raw, otherwise, prepare them beforehand.

2. Warm-up two deep bowls. Add the pasta evenly. Then decorate the bowls with the raw vegetables in parts until they are filled. It looks particularly nice if you don't mix the vegetables, but put them in different parts of the bowl. The vegetables in the bowl absorb a lot of broth and also release a lot of their own juice, which is why the end product tastes less intense than the broth from the stove. Now quickly bring the broth to a hot boil again and pass it through a sieve. Distribute the sieved broth evenly into the bowls until they are full to the brim. Then put the bean sprouts on the vegetables and put the meat on top.

HARD – 90+ MINUTES

TRADITIONAL RAMEN SOUP

INGREDIENTS FOR 4 PORTIONS

- 500g of pork loin or pork loin
- 100ml of soy sauce
- 500g of ramen noodles
- 4 cloves of garlic
- 3 spring onions
- 4 carrots
- 100g of bean sprouts
- 4 eggs
- 1 pinch pepper
- 1 pinch of salt
- 1 tbsp of sugar
- 4 shiitake mushroom or mushrooms
- 1 tbsp of chili flakes (your choice)
- 600ml of vegetable stock

PREPARATION

Total time: approx. 1 hour 45 minutes

1. Place the pressure cooker on the stove, add a dash of oil and sear the meat on all sides so that it gets to color. Then deglaze with the broth and add the soy sauce. Let everything cook for at least an hour with the lid closed.

2. In the meantime, you can cook the eggs hard and cut the vegetables into slices. Cut the onion into eighths. Add the sugar and the spices to the vegetables so that everything can go straight into the pot.

3. When the meat is cooked, you can take it out and put the pasta with the vegetables in the pot. Then carefully pull the meat apart with two forks so that there are small threads. When you're done, put the meat back in the pot. Stir again and serve.

VEGAN RAMEN SOUP

INGREDIENTS FOR 4 PORTIONS

- 250g of mie noodles, vegan
- 1 onion
- 5 garlic cloves
- ½ bundle of spring onions
- 14g shiitake mushroom (dried)
- 1,400ml of vegetable stock
- 2 tbsp of soy sauce
- 1 tbsp of miso paste (light)
- 1 teaspoon of ginger powder
- 2 tbsp of sesame oil for frying

For the vegetables:

- 6 carrots
- 2 pak choi
- 2 tbsp of miso paste (dark)
- 2 tbsp of maple syrup

- 2 tbsp of rice wine vinegar
- 1 tbsp of soy sauce
- 2 tbsp of vegetable oil

Moreover:

- 200g smoked
- 1 tbsp of food starch
- 1 shot of soy sauce
- 1 tbsp of sesame oil

PREPARATION

Total time: approx. 1 hour 50 minutes

1. Cut half of the onion and slice it roughly into strips, finely chop the garlic. Slice the spring onions and set the green part aside.
2. Heat the sesame oil in a large saucepan and fry the onions for 6 minutes. Add the white part of the spring onions, the garlic, and the ground ginger, and sauté for 2 minutes. Deglaze the onions with 200ml broth and loosen the roast on the bottom of the pot with a wooden spoon. Add the remaining broth, the soy sauce, and the dried mushrooms, and stir in. Bring the soup to a boil once, and then simmer on low heat with the lid closed for 1-2 hours. The longer the soup simmers, the more intense the taste becomes. Season the broth with soy sauce and add the miso paste. Finally, add the Mie noodles to the soup and let them cook in the soup until they have reached the desired bite resistance.
3. Preheat the oven to 220°C. Halve the Pak choi, cut the carrots into bite-size pieces. Mix the remaining ingredients into a sauce. Spread the sauce on the cut surface of the Pak Choi. Swirl the carrot pieces in the remaining sauce and place it on the baking sheet. Cook the carrots in the oven for 30-40 minutes. In the last 10 minutes, place the Pak choi on the tray with the cut surface facing up, and bake with it.
4. Dice the tofu and mix it with 1 tbsp. of starch. Heat the vegetable oil in a pan and fry the tofu all over for 10 minutes with sufficient oil until crispy. Finally, deglaze with a dash of soy sauce.
5. Spread the soup on bowls. Spread the tofu, Pak choi, and carrots over the pasta and garnish everything with the green part of the spring onions.

SPICY VEGETARIAN RAMEN

INGREDIENTS FOR 2 PORTIONS

- 180g of ramen noodles
- 2 cups of water
- 1 sheet of algae (kelp, large, or 5 - 10 strips)
- 1 handful of shiitake mushroom or other mushrooms, dried
- 2 tbsp of sesame oil
- 1 onion
- 2 cloves of garlic
- 2cm of ginger
- 1 tbsp of tomato paste
- 1 tbsp of sesame
- 2 tbsp of sake
- 3 tbsp of soy sauce
- 1 tbsp of mirin
- 2 cup of soy milk (soy drink, unsweetened)

- 1 pinch of pepper (white)
- ¼ tbsp of sea salt (ground)
- Chili powder or shichimi togarashi (chili spice mixture)
- 3 eggs
- Corn
- Cabbage
- Soy sauce
- Chili powder
- Some bean sprouts

PREPARATION

Total time: approx. 2 hours

1. Soak the mushrooms and seaweed in 2 cups of lukewarm water for 30 minutes.
2. In the meantime, you can dice the onion, dice the ginger and press the garlic.
3. Brown the sesame seeds in a hot dry pan and then grind them with a mortar. Then sauté this together with onion, ginger, and garlic in sesame oil, and color it red with tomato paste.
4. Bring the mushroom and seaweed broth to a boil and then remove the mushrooms and seaweed so that only the broth is left. Then set the broth aside.
5. Add the sake, soy sauce, and mirin to the onions, bring to a boil and then pour in soy milk and broth as needed. You have to vary something with the soy milk and the broth, depending on the amount you may have to add a little bit of both. Season with white pepper, salt, and chili spice and, if necessary, season with sake, soy sauce and mirin.
6. Also, prepare the toppings, hard boil, and peel, and then halve the eggs. Season the cabbage with chili powder and soy sauce and cook. Boil the corn and prepare other vegetables if necessary.
7. Finally, cook the noodles according to the package instructions, the best way to use ramen noodles here. Spaghetti is often used as an alternative, but I cannot imagine the taste.
8. When everything is ready, put the noodles in the bowls, distribute the hot broth and fill with toppings.

RAMEN WITH CHICKEN

INGREDIENTS FOR 6 PORTIONS

- 1 kg of chicken, a whole or chicken leg
- 2 cloves of garlic
- 1 piece of ginger (approx. 2 cm, peeled)
- 2 spring onion (cleaned)
- Sesame oil
- ½ bar of leek (cleaned)
- 3 carrots (peeled)
- Parsley
- 1 bay leaf
- Salt
- Some peppercorns
- Chili flakes
- Sriracha sauce
- Soy sauce
- 400g of noodles
- Some shiitake mushroom (optional)
- 6 eggs

PREPARATION

Total time: approx. 1 hour 50 minutes

1. Put the chicken in a saucepan with 1 spring onion, carrots, leek, parsley, bay leaf, peppercorns, salt, and chili flakes (to taste). Cover with water, bring to a boil and simmer in about 1 hour.

2. In the meantime, chop the white side of the second spring onion, the ginger, and the garlic as finely as possible and sauté in sesame oil on medium heat. Finely chopped mushrooms or similar can also be added.

3. Cut the green of the spring onion into rings.

4. If the spices in the sesame oil are well browned, deglaze with a generous portion of soy sauce and sriracha (as desired). Reduce the heat and let the soy sauce caramelize.

5. Remove the chicken from the saucepan and break it open slightly to allow it to evaporate faster. Pour the broth through a sieve and put it back into the pot without the vegetables.

6. Boil water in a small saucepan and add the eggs. Cook to taste for 8-10 minutes and chill well. Peel and cut in half.

7. Pour some of the broth into the pan with the spices, stir well to scrape everything off the floor and season the broth with the resulting seasoning mixture. Remove the meat from the chicken. Cook the pasta in the broth and arrange everything together. Serve sprinkled with the green of the spring onion.

CHASHU-MEN RAMEN

INGREDIENTS FOR 4 PORTIONS

- 1 boiling fowl
- 12cm of ginger
- 250ml of soy sauce (japanese)
- 500g of noodles
- 6 toes of garlic
- 1 onion
- 1 bar of leek
- 6 carrots
- 1 nori
- 100g of bean sprouts, fresh
- 4 eggs
- 6 spring onions
- 1 pinch of salt
- 1 pinch of pepper
- 1 tbsp of sugar

- 450g of pork belly or shoulder
- 2 tbsp of mirin (japanese cooking wine)
- 50ml of sake (japanese rice wine)
- 8 grains of pepper
- 1 tbsp of honey
- 1 tbsp of maple syrup
- Water
- Oil (for frying)

PREPARATION

Total time: approx. 1 hours 15 minutes + 3-4 hour for the broth

1. The recipe consists of two broths, so you should also wait until the taste to combine both. You will come to the second one later; first, go to the chicken broth:

2. Now add the following ingredients to a large saucepan:
   - The soup chicken
   - Three spring onions stick
   - Leek
   - A peeled onion
   - Four peeled cloves of garlic
   - Four carrots
   - A nori leaf
   - 4cm peeled ginger

3. Now that all the ingredients are in the pot, fill in enough water to cover the chicken, add salt, pepper and sugar and heat everything. Now the broth has to simmer on medium heat for 3-4 hours. If foam forms, skim it off so that the broth later becomes nice and clear.

4. When the cooking time is over, sieve the broth and set it aside. The contents of the sieve can be discarded.

5. Now that the chicken broth is ready, let's take a look at the meat and the second broth:

6. First, we peel the remaining two cloves of garlic and the remaining ginger and put both aside. Then we grab a saucepan, add oil and fry the meat on all sides over medium heat. Once this is done, we take out the meat, clean the pot and put it back on the stove at the same heat.

7. Now add the following ingredients to the pot:
   - Soy sauce
   - Mirin
   - Sake
   - Peppercorns
   - Maple syrup

- Honey

8. Stir everything well and bring to a boil. As soon as this is done, put the fried meat and the remaining ingredients, i.e. the peeled ginger, 2 spring onions and the cloves of garlic in the pot and fill it with enough boiling water until the meat is lightly covered. Now put the lid on the pot and let everything simmer on moderate heat for one to one and a half hours. Turn the meat every now and then.

9. In that time, you can cook the eggs hard. As soon as the meat is ready, we take it out of the pot, cut it into slices and sieve this broth.

10. Now that we have both broths ready, you can pour them both together and bring them to a boil again so that the broth is nice and hot. At this point, it is also advisable to season everything and, if necessary, season with soy sauce and/or rice wine. Now we're almost ready to eat, just boil and drain the noodles, rinse the bean sprouts, and cut a few raw carrots into thin strips.

11. With that, everything should be ready and ready to serve.

12. Put some of the vegetable strips, the bean sprouts and the pasta in a bowl, fill up with the hot broth (this is enough to heat the vegetables) and with a few slices of meat, half an egg and one Garnish with a few spring onion rings.

JAPANESE NOODLES SOUP WITH CHICKEN BROTH

INGREDIENTS FOR 4 PORTIONS

- 1 pork loin (pork fillet), in one piece, approximately (approx.) 500g
- 1 soup chicken (frozen)
- 1 piece of ginger root, approx. 8 cm
- Water
- 100ml soy sauce, japanese
- 100ml rice wine or sake
- 500g of soup noodles
- 4 cloves of garlic
- 1 bar of leek
- 4 carrots
- 1 nori sheets
- 100g of bean sprouts (fresh)
- 3 eggs
- 3 spring onions
- Salt and pepper
- 1 tablespoon of sugar

PREPARATION

Total time: approx. 1 hours 45 minutes + 3-4 hours for the broth

The broth:

1. Mix the soup chicken with a stick of leek, an onion, three to four cloves of garlic, five centimeters of ginger, a pinch of salt, three to four carrots and a handful of algae (optional) in cold water. Add enough water to cover the chicken completely. (Choose pot size so that everything plus two to three liters of water fits in well - a five-liter pot is ideal).

2. Bring to a slow simmer, and let it simmer for at least 3-4 hours. The broth becomes even more delicious with cooking times of 6 - 8 hours. If there is foam, you can skim it off, but it's unnecessary.

3. The broth should not boil too much - just simmer gently. The longer this broth cooks the better. Then sieve the broth. I do not use boiled parts. It is better to use a good real soup chicken, not a chicken.

The loin:

1. Briefly sear the pork loin in a pan on all sides until it is slightly brown. Don't fry too long - just lightly brown. Then put in a saucepan and pour in 100ml soy sauce (I use Kikkoman because it is naturally brewed) and 50ml to 100ml rice wine (I use Chinese rice wine). Add 1 tablespoon of sugar, a sliced spring onion (with the green and only a little of the onion) and 3cm of grated fresh ginger. Pour in a little water so that the loin is almost completely covered with liquid. Then bring the liquid to a simmer. Let it simmer again slightly.

2. After 40 minutes, take the loin out of the liquid and set aside. Then cut the loin into slices (approx. 2 - 3 mm thick) before it comes into the soup.

3. The loin should come from a good butcher - there are amazing quality differences. A good loin is very tender and juicy after this procedure, not tough and dry.

The eggs:

1. Cook four eggs hard and peel them. Put the eggs in the loin broth and simmer for 10 minutes. Turn again and again so that they are evenly browned by the brew. When they're done, cut them in half and set them aside.

The pasta:

1. You can make your own noodles while the broths are cooking (recipes for this can be found in this book) or use Chinese soup noodles from the Asian shop. I've had very good experiences with quick noodles, and even spaghetti in them tastes very good. If you have a well-stocked Asian shop, you may even get ramen noodles or fresh ramen noodles.

2. According to the instructions, always cook the pasta strictly hard, not too soft.

The soup:

1. When the chicken broth is ready, put it in a saucepan with the loin broth and season with a few tablespoons of soy sauce and another shot of rice wine. You can add salt, but the soy sauce should actually provide enough salt. Then let everything boil again. You can also add water, depending on how strong or diluted you want the soup. I leave the broth pure without adding water. When the soup cooks, all other ingredients should be ready for the next step, especially the pasta.

Garnish:

1. Scald the bean sprouts with hot water in a sieve. Cut the green of two spring onions into rings. Cut small strips (approx. 2 x 3 cm) from the nori sheets.

The finish:

1. Put the soup in a bowl and add enough pasta, so that the pasta reaches just below the surface.

2. Add two or three slices of the loin. The loin can be sprinkled with coarse pepper.

3. Place half an egg on the edge of the shell with the egg yolk facing up.

4. Sprinkle a small handful of sprouts and spring onions over it and then add the nori leaf.

5. Enjoy the sight of the soup. Eating with chopsticks and sipping the broth loudly - it tastes best this way.

Note:

- The cooked loin can also be placed on a bowl of rice and poured over with the loin broth. Also very tasty as an alternative dish.

The soup is actually not complex, but it takes a lot of time because all the ingredients have to be cooked for a long time to develop a unique taste. It really pays off not to get hectic with the broth, and allow it the necessary cooking time. The recipe is a kind of basic recipe. The broth can be further refined (e.g. with algae or dashi) or pork bones can also be cooked alongside the chicken. A whole lot is also suitable as an inlay for the soup - just experiment or check out what others are doing online.

The soup is very invigorating and also amazingly filling.

NOODLES SOUP WITH CHICKEN

INGREDIENTS FOR 6 PORTIONS

For the broth:

- 1 boiling fowl
- 4 carrots
- 1 leek
- 4 cloves of garlic
- 3cm of ginger root
- 1 pinch of salt

For the brew:

- 100ml of soy sauce
- 80ml of sake or chinese wine, in need gin or vodka
- 2 spring onions
- 3cm of ginger root

Moreover:

- 4 eggs
- 500g of ramen noodles (spaghetti broken through 3 times is sufficient in an emergency)
- Pepper
- Some spring onion (cut into rings, for decoration)

PREPARATION

Total time: approx. 1 hours 30 minutes + 3-4 hours for the broth

The broth:

1. Gently boil the soup chicken, carrots, leeks, cloves of garlic, and ginger in salted water for 3 - 4 hours.
2. Lift the chicken out of the broth and let it cool slightly. Detach the meat from the bones and cut it into edible pieces.
3. Boil and peel the eggs hard.

For the brew:

1. Heat in a saucepan with a lid of soy sauce, sake or similar. Cut 2 spring onions into small rings and add small ginger. Fold in the meat, and then simmer everything on a low flame for about 10 minutes with the lid closed. Insert the eggs and turn more often in the brew. Let everything simmer for another 10 minutes.
2. Cook the pasta bite-proof and pour off according to the instructions.
3. Remove the leek and garlic from the broth and discard. Cut the carrots into slices and set them aside. Pour the broth through a sieve into another large saucepan to get a nice clear broth. Pepper the broth.
4. Lift the meat and eggs out of the broth. Stir the broth from soy sauce into the broth.
5. Provide bowls. Pour in the broth, add the noodles, insert 2 halves of a cut egg, put on the meat and decorate with spring onion rings. Add the carrot slices. If necessary, soy sauce can also be added.

NOODLES SOUP WITH CHICKEN THIGH

INGREDIENTS FOR 4 PORTIONS

- 400g of wheat flour
- 180ml of mineral water (cold)
- 5g of salt
- 4 chicken legs
- 1 spring onion
- 1 carrot
- 1 small chinese cabbage
- 100g of bean sprouts
- 500ml of water
- 15g dashi no moto (dashi stock base made of bonito fish powder)
- 3 tbsp of soy sauce
- 3 tbsp of mirin
- 1 tbsp of sugar
- 2 tbsp of oil (tasteless)

PREPARATION

Total time approx. 1 hour 45 minutes

1. For the Udon noodles, mix the flour with the salt and the cold mineral water until a firm dough is formed. Ideally, it is done with a kneading machine for 5 minutes or until the thickness of the pasta is reached. They have to be firm; otherwise, they will fall apart in the hot water. Let the dough cool for 30 minutes.

2. In the meantime, bone the chicken drumsticks and leave them on the skin. Cut the soft cabbage portion from the top of the Chinese cabbage and the hard stalk below. Cut the middle part into bite-size pieces. Wash the bean sprouts, remove dry leaves and roots from the spring onions, wash and cut into thin diagonal slices. Peel the carrots and cut them into thin strips, preferably with an asparagus peeler. Again, it should be cut into bite-size pieces. Roll out the Udon dough and cut into strips of approx. 5mm thick pasta in a pasta machine. If you do not have a pasta machine, you have to fold the dough three to four times (dust well with flour so that it does not stick) and then cut into 5mm strips with the largest knife.

3. Heat soy sauce, mirin, water, dashi no moto, sugar, and half of the oil in a saucepan. Add the carrot and Chinese cabbage and simmer for about 5 minutes. Let the other half of the oil heat up in a pan and fry the chicken legs with the skin side down for about 5 minutes (or until the skin is brown), then turn and fry.

4. Pour the pasta water as usual and put the Udon noodles in deep plates and place the soybean sprouts and the spring onion rings on them, put the hot soup on the noodles and top the whole thing with the fried chicken drumstick, from the pan onto a piece of kitchen paper (to absorb the excess fat) and then cut into bite-size pieces with a sharp butcher knife.

VEGETABLE AND MUSHROOM PAN

INGREDIENTS FOR 4 PORTIONS

For the marinade:

- 3 tbsp of soy sauce
- 1 tbsp of honey
- 1 tbsp of sesame oil
- 1 clove of garlic
- 1 small piece of ginger root
- Chili
- Lemon pepper

Moreover:

- 200g of beefsteak
- 250g of udon noodles
- 40g of shiitake mushroom, dried
- 250g of mushrooms, brown
- 1 bunch spring onions

- 200g of sugar snap
- 250g of paprika
- 6 tbsp of soy sauce
- 1 tbsp of oil
- 1 tbsp of sesame

PREPARATION

Total time approx. 3 hours 40 minutes

1. Mix the ingredients for the marinade. Cut the steak into fine strips and let it marinate for 2-3 hours.

2. Let the shiitake mushrooms soak for 1 hour according to the package instructions.

3. In the meantime, wash and prepare the vegetables. Clean the mushrooms and cut them into slices or cubes. Cut the spring onions into rings. Cut the bell pepper into cubes. Blanch the sugar snap peas briefly in boiling water. If fresh ones are used, first pull off the fine threads on the side with a sharp knife.

4. Cook the Udon noodles according to the package instructions (approx. 13 minutes) and drain well.

5. Sear the meat for 1 minute and remove from the pan. Then sear the peppers until firm and add the mushrooms. When the mushrooms are well browned, add sugar snap peas, spring onions, and pasta and stir everything well.

6. Add the meat again. Add 6 tablespoons of soy sauce and stir well again.

7. Finally, sprinkle 1-2 tablespoons of sesame over the food, depending on your taste.

RICE NOODLES AND CHICKEN

INGREDIENTS FOR 2 PORTIONS

- 150g of rice noodles (japanese)
- 2m in size of chicken breasts
- 1 tbsp of rapeseed oil or sesame oil
- 1 carrot
- 1 bar of leek
- 8 mushrooms (fresh)
- 150g spring onions
- Chili pepper (fresh)
- ½ glass of bamboo shoot
- 2 toes of garlic
- 1 piece of ginger (approx. 1 cm x 1 cm x 1 cm)
- 1 chili pepper (red, dried)
- 4 tbsp of soy sauce light)
- 2 tbsp of fish sauce
- 50 ml of chicken broth
- 1 tbsp of coriander seeds
- 1 tbsp of sesame (lien ying goma), toasted
- Black pepper

PREPARATION

Total time: approx. 1 hour 45 minutes

1. Cut the chicken breasts into strips approx. 1cm thick with 3 tablespoons of light soy sauce (Please be very careful with this, chicken breasts are often of different sizes. Make sure that the meat "looks marinated"), a clove of garlic and mix with a teaspoon of toasted sesame seeds, and then put in a bowl.

2. Letting it simmer for an hour should be the most pragmatic case, but for everyday life, it is enough to keep the meat in the sauce while slicing vegetables.

3. Then heat the rapeseed or sesame oil in a wok or wok pan. With sesame oil, I advise extreme caution when dosing, since it is very aromatic. Sauté finely chopped garlic, also finely chopped ginger as well as the dried chili and coriander seeds before frying the meat together with the soy sauce for approx. 2-3 minutes. I personally just break open the pod and put the seeds in the oil. It would also be conceivable to place the pod completely in the oil and remove it before adding the meat. In this way, the oil is pleasantly flavored and the sharpness is limited.

4. Take the meat out again and set it aside. Add the leek rings, carrot slices, the mushrooms, and the chili peppers (I take it very mildly, peppers are an excellent alternative) in the remaining oil and steam for a few minutes. Then deglaze with a dash of soy sauce and 2 tablespoons of fish sauce. Then mix in the bamboo saplings and spring onions, let them warm briefly and add the meat again.

5. With the vegetables, the soy and fish sauce, the dish should already have developed enough liquid. To curb and round off the taste, I recommend a little chicken broth. I would avoid salt for this dish because the soy sauce is already very salty.

6. Shortly before serving, mix in the rice noodles that were previously prepared according to the package description. Sprinkle some sesame seeds on the plate.

7. Tip: If you have no experience with fish sauce, please dose it a little more sparingly and do not let the smell deter you. This flies in the pot after a few seconds.

SUKIYAKI

INGREDIENTS FOR 4 PORTIONS

- 250g of tofu
- 150g of glass noodles (japanese)
- 10 shiitake mushrooms
- 100g of mushrooms (enoki mushrooms) or oyster mushrooms
- 200g of herbs (shungiku or salads chrysanthemum) or spinach leaves
- 2 bars of leek
- 400g of chinese cabbage
- 600g of entrecote (cut into 2mm thin slices)
- 3 tbsp of vegetable oil
- 120ml of soy sauce (japanese)
- 120ml of mirin
- 4 eggs (fresh)
- 2 tbsp of sugar

PREPARATION

Total time: approx. 2 hours 20 minutes

1. Put the tofu briefly in cold water, drain and pat dry carefully. Cut into 16 pieces. Boil the noodles in plenty of water for about 5 minutes and drain. For dried shiitake mushrooms, pour boiling water over them and let them soak in the water for 20 minutes. Remove the stems as they can be very hard. Wipe the mushrooms with a cloth, leave part of it whole and cut part into triangles. Wash the Enoki and remove the brown section. Clean and wash the Shungiku.

2. Clean and wash the Chinese cabbage and cut the leaves into pieces about 10cm long. Bring water to a boil in a saucepan. Blanch the cabbage for about 5 minutes, drain and press a little so that it is not too watery. Remove the leek from roots and green leaves and wash. Cut diagonally into pieces about 5cm long. It is best to cut the entrecote thinly if it has been briefly frozen. Decorate the ingredients including entrecote on a large platter. Add chopsticks or forks.

3. For the sauces, bring the soy sauce, mirin, and sugar to a short boil in a saucepan. Remove 150ml and put it in a jug. Add 50ml of water to the remaining sauce and put the diluted sauce in a second jug.

4. Place a fresh, raw egg in each bowl and whisk. Place a hotplate or gas burner with a Sukiyaki pot, available in an Asian shop, or a roasting pan on the table and heat. Add oil and briefly fry several slices of meat. Add about half of the undiluted sauce. Add some of the vegetables and some tofu. When the sauce is boiling, add a portion of the glass noodles and cook with tofu, meat, and vegetables for 6-8 minutes.

5. Each person at the table serves himself with chopsticks or forks from the Sukiyaki pot. The meat and other ingredients are briefly dipped in the egg before they are eaten.

6. You determine the rhythm in which to eat and put meat, vegetables and other ingredients in the pot. Even while it is cooking, you can use the pot and add new ingredients. Do not put too many ingredients in the pot at once. Top up the sauce again and again during preparation. First, use undiluted and then the diluted sauce so that the taste does not become too intense. (Approx. 700 Kcal per serving).

SZECHUAN PEPPER CHICKEN

INGREDIENTS FOR 4 PORTIONS

- 3 tbsp of szechuan pepper
- 2 cloves of garlic
- 1 tbsp of ginger (chopped)
- 3 tbsp of food starch
- 2 tbsp of soy sauce (dark)
- 600g of chicken thighs
- 100g of ramen noodles
- 3 tbsp of vegetable oil
- 1 onion
- 1 pepper (yellow)
- 1 bell pepper (red)
- 100g of sweet peas
- 80ml of chicken broth

PREPARATION

Total time: approx. 2 hours 40 minutes

1. Roast the Szechuan pepper without oil until it starts to smell. Then mortar and mix with the chopped cloves of garlic, ginger, soy sauce, and cornstarch.

2. Skin the chicken legs, remove the meat from the bones and cut into strips. Mix well with the previously made marinade and leave covered for two hours in the fridge.

3. Thinly strip the two peppers, cut the onion into rings. Cook the pasta in boiling salted water and drain.

4. Fry the chicken in portions in hot vegetable oil. Remove from the wok or pan and cook the peppers, the onion rings, and the peas in the roast stock for two to three minutes, stirring constantly. If canned peas are used, then let the temperature rise briefly at the end. Add the chicken broth and bring to a boil. The sauce thickens due to the starch in the marinade. Add the chicken strips and the pasta to the hot mixture and mix. It can then be served immediately.

Made in the USA
Las Vegas, NV
03 December 2024

12529661R00104